D0885286

GETTING THINGS DONE
KEYS TO A SUCCESSFUL BUSINESS

INSIGHT PUBLISHING
SEVIERVILLE, TENNESSEE

GETTING THINGS DONE

KEYS TO A SUCCESSFUL BUSINESS

Disclaimer: This book is a compilation of ideas from numerous experts who have each contributed a chapter. As such, the views expressed in each chapter are of those who were interviewed and not necessarily of the interviewer or Insight Publishing.

Published by Insight Publishing Company
P.O. Box 4189
Sevierville, Tennessee 37864

10 9 8 7 6 5 4 3 2

Printed in the United States of America

ISBN: 978-1-60013- 094-1

Table of Contents

A Message from the Publisher

Being able to get things done is about more than being an efficient, industrious self-starter. It includes being organized—mentally and in the workplace. It's about emptying your inbox, getting control of your schedule, and accomplishing your tasks.

I wondered how the busy, successful people I knew were able to get things done and I began to search for some answers. The result is this book and you will see why these men and women were asked to share their secrets.

I asked questions like, "What keeps you focused?" "How do you think technology factors into the theme of getting things done?" "What are the key areas of your plan that you consider in order to effectively manage life and work?" and I received some very interesting and informative answers. I think you'll agree.

When you read this book and incorporate the tools these authors have used to get things done, you'll wonder how you ever got along without them. The ideas you'll gain from this educational collection of interviews will help move you forward and enable you to take control of your work life and your personal life. If you need that extra bit of encouragement, that one piece of the puzzle to help you get things done in your own life, this is the book for you.

Wait no longer—turn the page and start your journey. You'll be glad you did!

Interviews conducted by:
David E. Wright
President, International Speakers Network

Chapter 1

ED KUGLER

David Wright (Wright)
Today we're talking with Ed Kugler. Ed is an experienced business coach and an accomplished inspirational speaker with over three decades leading people in unique situations. He brings his unique style and background to life with real stories from Vietnam to small business and to the Boardrooms of Fortune 50 companies. He is a former Marine sniper in the Vietnam War and he authored *Dead Center—A Marine Sniper's Two-Year Odyssey in the Vietnam War.* He rose from truck mechanic to Vice President of Compaq Computer without the benefit of a college degree. He is President of his own company, author of five books, and a husband, father, and grandfather.

Ed, welcome to *Getting Things Done.*

Ed Kugler (Kugler)
Thank you.

Wright
Ed, tell us about your business background and how you got where you are.

1

Kugler

My life is pretty unique. I joined the Marines at seventeen, right out of high school. I spent two years in Vietnam as a Marine sniper and that's where I learned the most about leadership. I came home and worked as a mechanic, truck driver, and dispatcher and then went into management. I spent ten years in trucking and parlayed that into a corporate job at Frito Lay.

I was promoted five times my first six years with Frito and spent thirteen years with them before transferring to Pepsi Cola for three years. From there I moved to Compaq Computer where I was Vice President of Worldwide Logistics. I spent three years there and left to start my own firm, Direct Hit Inc. where I provide help in turning bad operations around and coaching people to change.

Wright

Wow, that is unique background for sure. Did you work college in there somewhere?

Kugler

Well, no, I didn't. My wife got me to try college and I did fine for a guy who graduated from high school with a 1.9 GPA. I attended a branch of Kent State for a couple years worth of credits and was attending when the shootings took place. I wasn't there that day but in the classes after that day the professors made me sick. I left there with a chip on my shoulder about education and decided I'd do it my way.

Wright

So you were the VP of a company like Compaq and did it with no college degree. Tell us your secret.

Kugler

Well, there's no secret. The single biggest thing I did was take advantage of every opportunity I was given. I looked for areas that needed fixing and I volunteered to fix them. I can say I never really aspired to any particular position, I just delivered results in whatever I was asked to do.

Wright

So how did you do that?

Kugler

I started by deciding to make a difference in everything I did. That just means leaving it better than I found it. I learned in Vietnam as a Marine sniper that I had to take charge of whatever I did if I was going to survive. So first off, I made a commitment to make things better. That means you know where you're going.

The second thing is to know straight up that nothing happens without people. You will only succeed long-term with people. A majority of people today use people. I learned in 'Nam that doesn't work.

Wright

So talk more about the people aspect of getting things done in business.

Kugler

It's all about leadership. Whether you're at the top of the corporation or your small business or you're a front line supervisor, it's about leadership. When you see problems like Enron, on the large side you see leadership issues. When you see Iraq, you see leadership issues just like in Vietnam; it translates all the way down to each one of us in businesses large or small. We must lead ourselves and our organizations, regardless of the position we hold.

Wright

So leaders are the key to getting things done in business?

Kugler

That's right. Leaders have to set the direction. People won't pay the price if they can't see the promise. Jim Rohn said that and he's right. I've seen it in Vietnam and in corporate America. Leadership is the key to success whether you're leading a group of people or yourself.

Wright

Exactly how do leaders "get things done"?

Kugler

The first thing a good leader does is to create a compelling vision or direction. Second, good leaders recognize that they must engage the whole individual—the entire person. By that I mean they recognize that they must engage the head, heart, and hands to really get things done and be successful.

Wright

I haven't heard that one before, will you elaborate?

Kugler

Sure. You realize that people come to you with the ability to perform, work "the hands." Take McDonald's for instance. They have systematized their business to the point that about all someone needs to work there is their "hands"—minimal skills and that's it. Then you take Compaq Computer where I worked; they engaged the "hands" as well as the "head." Tech businesses require a degree of intellect that McDonald's on the surface doesn't. So there is the "head."

But the real key to productivity and getting things done is for leaders to engage the "heart"—the passion of a person. Few businesses do this well at all. In the case of Compaq they engaged all three when Rod Canion was there as the founder and all the start-up excitement was alive. When they threw him out they began to lose the passion—the heart—of the people and you can see where that led down the road. Successful companies have leaders who engage all three key elements of people.

Wright

Well now, that's an interesting concept. Does it relate to businesses large and small?

Kugler

By all means. It doesn't matter. It worked in Vietnam leading Marine snipers and it works in corporate America or the downtown café. It works when leaders recognize me as an individual—as a whole person and not an "asset" or someone to be told what to do. As an individual, I felt good and I felt like I "belonged" when someone recognized me in this way. People want to belong to something bigger than themselves. I voluntarily stayed in Vietnam for two years, not only one year, because I had that sense of "belonging." It's a simple concept and good leaders know how to engage the whole person.

Wright

What comes next in our journey to "get things done"?

Kugler

The third thing is that once you know where you're going and engage the whole person, you create an environment where it is safe to tell you you're all wet. Now, it has to be done appropriately in time and place but it has to be okay to tell you when I think you're wrong. For people to be productive and belong they have to be able to tell you the truth. You see, as a people we should have learned this in Vietnam and now in Iraq but the Enrons are everywhere out there today. Leaders create safe environments and get the truth.

Wright

I can see that and I'm not sure we have learned those lessons but go on.

Kugler

The last thing is execution. Something has to get done. You have to take action. Leaders set the course and follow up to see that results are delivered. That means they make it clear with their followers what is expected and when. They gain agreement on the desired end, they see that people have the resources needed to deliver the result, and then they get out of the way. But, they follow up and hold people accountable. We all do what is expected, right or wrong we do, so leaders make that clear and provide accountability.

Wright

Is it that simple?

Kugler

Well, it's that simple to understand. Like everything else, doing it is another matter but it shouldn't be hard, it should be who you are as a leader. It's all a matter of knowing where you're going, creating a vision for others to follow, engaging the whole person, creating safe environments, and executing relentlessly. You have to remember that your habits have to support your vision or your vision is nothing more than a daydream.

Wright

That's fascinating and you've had some interesting experiences over the past three decades to back it up. Do you find it common out there in business today?

Kugler

Not at all. Personally, I saw the changes beginning to take place in the mid to late eighties. After two years in Vietnam as a Marine sniper I spent hours, days, and weeks, maybe months observing people both good and bad. It was a matter of survival obviously. So I do a lot of observing, I'm a student of leadership; it's almost a hobby with me. What I observed in leaders was a growing selfishness, looking out for number one, as we became a free agent society in the nineties. Today in almost every organization I work with, the gap between the senior leaders and the workers doing the work of the business is so wide, it's like trying to run and jump the Grand Canyon.

Wright

Unfortunately I think you're right. What can leaders do in business today to keep getting things done?

Kugler

They have to be true to their principles and those principles have to be like the Three Musketeers—"All for one, and one for all." It sounds corny but leaders have to act for the good of the whole. Then the four steps: shared vision, engaging the whole person, safe environments, and execution. The key is to understand that execution is the link between your vision and your results. If you don't plan it, do it, follow up, and make course corrections, it is not going to happen.

All actions need to have people's names on them and those people need to be held accountable for delivering results. That is how you get things done.

Wright

Well Ed, it's been interesting and I know your ideas will be of value to our listeners and readers.

Kugler

Thanks very much. It's been my pleasure. Always remember, what we do every day is what we believe, all the rest is just talk.

About the Author

ED KUGLER is an accomplished inspirational speaker with over three decades leading people and businesses to change for the better. He brings his unique style and background to life with real stories from Vietnam to the Boardroom. He is a former Marine sniper in the Vietnam War and authored *Dead Center—A Marine Sniper's Two-Year Odyssey in the Vietnam War.* He rose from truck mechanic to Vice President of Compaq Computer without the benefit of a college degree. He is President of his own company, author of five books, and a husband, father, and grandfather.

Ed Kugler
Direct Hit, Inc.
P.O. Box 190
Big Arm, MT 59910
Phone: 866.725.5506
E-mail: edkugler@nomorebs.com
www.nomorebs.com
www.edkugler.com

Chapter 2

DR. KEN BLANCHARD

David E. Wright (Wright)

Few people have created a positive impact on the day-to-day management of people and companies more than Dr. Kenneth Blanchard, who is known around the world simply as Ken, a prominent, gregarious, sought-after author, speaker, and business consultant. Ken is universally characterized by friends, colleagues, and clients as one of the most insightful, powerful, and compassionate men in business today. Ken's impact as a writer is far-reaching. His phenomenal best-selling book, *The One Minute Manager®*, co-authored with Spencer Johnson, has sold more than 13 million copies worldwide and has been translated into more than twenty-five languages. Ken is Chairman and Chief Spiritual Officer of the Ken Blanchard Companies. The organization's focus is to energize organizations around the world with customized training in bottom line business strategies based on the simple yet powerful principles inspired by Ken's best-selling books.

Dr. Blanchard, welcome to *Getting Things Done*!

Dr. Ken Blanchard (Blanchard)
Well, it's nice to talk to you, David. It's good to be here.

Wright
I must tell you that preparing for your interview took quite a bit more time than usual. The scope of your life's work and your business, the Ken Blanchard Companies, would make for a dozen fascinating interviews. Before we dive into the specifics of some of your projects and strategies, will you give our readers a brief synopsis of your life—how you came to be the Ken Blanchard that we all know and respect?

Blanchard
Well, I'll tell you, David, I think life is what you do when you are planning on doing something else. I think that was John Lennon's line. I never intended to do what I have been doing. In fact, all my professors in college told me that I couldn't write. I wanted to do college work, which I did, and they said, "You had better be an administrator." So I decided I was going to be a Dean of Students. I got provisionally accepted into my master's degree program and then provisionally accepted at Cornell, because I never could take any of those standardized tests.

I took the college boards four times and finally got 502 in English. I don't have a test-taking mind. I ended up in a university in Athens, Ohio, in 1966 as an Administrative Assistant to the Dean of the Business School. When I got there he said, "Ken, I want you to teach a course. I want all my deans to teach." I had never thought about teaching because they said I couldn't write, and teachers had to publish. He put me in the manager's department. I've taken enough bad courses in my day and I wasn't going to teach one. I really prepared and had a wonderful time with the students. I got chosen as one of the top ten teachers on the campus coming out of the chute. I just had a marvelous time. A colleague by the name of Paul Hersey was chairman of the management department. He wasn't real friendly to me initially because the Dean had led me into his department, but I heard he was a great teacher. He taught organizational behavior and leadership. So I said, "Can I sit in on your course next semester?" And he said, "Nobody audits my courses. If you want to take it for credit, you're welcome." I couldn't believe it. I had a doctoral degree and he wanted me to take his course for credit, so I signed up. The registrar didn't know what to do with me because I already had a doctorate, but I wrote the papers and took the course, and it was great. In June 1967, Hersey came into my office and said, "Ken, I've been teaching in this field for ten years. I think I'm better than anybody, but I can't write. I'm a nervous wreck, and I'd love to write a textbook with somebody. Would you write one with me?" I said, "We ought to be a great team. You can't write and I'm not supposed to be able to, so let's do it!" Thus began this great career of writing and teaching. We wrote a textbook called *Management of Organizational Behavior: Utilizing Human Resources.* It just came out in its eighth edition last year and has sold more than any other textbook in that area over the years. It's been nearly thirty-five years since that book came out. I quit my administrative job, became a professor, and ended up working my way up the ranks. I got a sabbatical leave and went to California for one year twenty-five years ago. I ended up meeting Spencer Johnson at a cocktail party. He wrote children's books, a wonderful series called *Value Tales for Kids including, The Value of Courage: The Story of Jackie Robinson and The Value of Believing In Yourself: The Story Louis Pasteur.* My wife, Margie, met him first and said, "You guys ought to write a children's book for managers because they won't read anything else." That was my introduction to Spencer. So, *The One Minute Manager* was really a kid's book for big people. That is a long way from saying that my career was well planned.

Wright

Ken, what and/or who were your early influences in the areas of business, leadership and success? In other words, who shaped you in your early years?

Blanchard

My father had a great impact on me. He was retired as an admiral in the Navy and had a wonderful philosophy. I remember when I was elected to president of the seventh grade, and I came home all pumped up. My father said, "Son, it's great that you're the president of the seventh grade, but now that you have that leadership position, don't ever use it." He said, "Great leaders are followed because people respect them and like them, not because they have power." That was a wonderful lesson for me early on. He was just a great model for me. I got a lot from him. Then I had this wonderful opportunity in the mid 1980's to write a book with Norman Vincent Peale. He wrote *The Power of Positive Thinking.* I met him when he was 86 years old and we were asked to write a book on ethics together, *The Power of Ethi-*

cal Management: Integrity Pays, You Don't Have to Cheat to Win. It didn't matter what we were writing together, I learned so much from him, and he just kind of built off the positive stuff I learned from my mother. My mother, when I was born, said that I laughed before I cried, I danced before I walked, and I smiled before I frowned. So that, on top of Norman Vincent Peale, really impacted me as I focused on what I could do to train leaders. How do you make them positive? How do you make them realize that it's not about them, it's about who they are serving. It's not about their position. It's about what they can do to help other people win. So, I'd say my mother and father, then Norman Vincent Peale, had a tremendous impact on me.

Wright

I can imagine. I read a summary of your undergraduate and graduate degrees. I assumed you studied business administration, marketing management, and related courses. Instead, at Cornell you studied government and philosophy. You received your master's from Colgate in sociology and counseling and your Ph.D. from Cornell in educational administration and leadership. Why did you choose this course of study? How has it affected your writing and consulting?

Blanchard

Well, again, it wasn't really well planned out. I originally went to Colgate to get a master's degree in education because I was going to be a Dean of Students over men. I had been a government major, and I was a government major because it was the best department at Cornell in the Liberal Arts School. It was exciting. We would study what the people were doing at the league governments. And then, the Philosophy Department was great. I just loved the philosophical arguments. I wasn't a great student in terms of getting grades, but I'm a total learner. I would sit there and listen, and I would really soak it in. When I went over to Colgate and got in these education courses, they were awful. They were boring. The second week, I was sitting at the bar at the Colgate Inn saying, "I can't believe I've been here two years for this." It's just the way the Lord works—sitting next to me in the bar was a young sociology professor who had just gotten his Ph.D. at Illinois. He was staying at the Inn. I was moaning and groaning about what I was doing, and he said, "Why don't you come and major with me in sociology? It's really exciting." I said, "I can do that?" He said, "Yes." I knew they would probably let me do whatever I wanted the first week. Suddenly, I switched out of education and went with

Warren Ramshaw. He had a tremendous impact on me. He retired a few years ago as the leading professor at Colgate in the Arts and Sciences, and got me interested in leadership and organizations. That's why I got a master's in sociology. The reason I went into educational administration and leadership? It was a doctoral program I could get into, because I knew the guy heading up the program. He said, "The greatest thing about Cornell is that you will be in a School of Education. It's not very big, so you don't have to take many education courses, and you can take stuff all over the place." There was a marvelous man by the name of Don McCarty, who ended up going on to be the Dean of the School of Education, Wisconsin. He had an impact on my life, but I was always just searching around. My mission statement is: to be a loving teacher and example of simple truths that helps myself and others to awaken the presence of God in our lives. The reason I mention "God" is that I believe the biggest addiction in the world is the human ego; but I'm really into simple truth. I used to tell people I was trying to get the B.S. out of the behavioral sciences.

Wright

I can't help but think when you mentioned your father, and how he just bottomed lined it for you about leadership.

Blanchard

Yes.

Wright

A man named Paul Myers, in Texas, years and years ago when I went to a conference down there, said, "David, if you think you're a leader and you look around, and no one is following you, you're just out for a walk."

Blanchard

Well, you'd get a kick; I'm just reaching over to pick up a picture of Paul Myers on my desk. He's a good friend, and he's a part of our Center for FaithWalk Leadership, where we're trying to challenge and equip people to lead like Jesus. It's non-profit, and I tell people I'm not an evangelist because we've got enough trouble with the Christians we have. We don't need any more new ones. But, this is a picture of Paul on top of a mountain, and then another picture below of him under the sea with stingrays. It says, "Attitude is everything. Whether you're on the top of the mountain or the bottom of the sea, true happiness is achieved by accepting God's promises, and by having a biblically positive frame of mind. Your attitude is everything." Isn't that something?

Wright

He's a fine, fine man. He helped me tremendously. In keeping with the theme of our book, *Getting Things Done,* I wanted to get a sense from you about your own success journey. Many people know you best from *The One Minute Manager* books you coauthored with Spencer Johnson. Would you consider these books as a high water mark for you, or have you defined success for yourself in different terms?

Blanchard

Well, you know *The One Minute Manager* was an absurdly successful book, so quickly I found I couldn't take credit for it. That was when I really got on my own spiritual journey and started to try to find out what the real meaning of life and success was. That's been a wonderful journey for me because I think, David, the problem with most people is they think their self-worth is a function of their performance plus the opinion of others. The minute you think that is what your self-worth is, every day your self-worth is up for grabs because your performance is going to fluctuate on a day-to-day basis. People are fickle. Their opinions are going to go up and down. You need to ground your self-worth in the unconditional love that God has ready for us, and that really grew out of the unbelievable success of *The One Minute Manager.* When I started to realize where all that came from, that's how I got involved in this ministry that I mentioned. Paul Myers is a part of it. As I started to read the Bible, I realized that everything I've ever written about, or taught, Jesus did. You know, he did it with twelve incompetent guys that he hired. The only guy with much education was Judas, and he was his only turnover problem.

Wright

Right.

Blanchard

It was a really interesting thing. What I see in people is not only do they think their self-worth is a function of their performance plus the opinion of others, but they measure their success on the amount of accumulation of wealth, on recognition, power, and status. I think those are nice success items. There's nothing wrong with those, as long as you don't define your life by that. What I think you need to focus on rather than success is what Bob Buford, in his book, *Half-time,* calls significance. He talks about moving from success to significance. I think the opposite of accumulation of wealth is generosity.

I wrote a book called *The Generosity Factor* with Truett Cathy, who is the founder of Chick-fil-A, one of the most generous men I've ever met in my life. I thought we needed to have a model of generosity. It's not only your treasure, but it's time, talent. Truett and I added *touch* as a fourth one. The opposite of recognition is service. I think you become an adult when you realize you're here to serve rather than to be served. Finally, the opposite of power and status is loving relationships. Mother Teresa as an example, she could have cared less about recognition, power, and status because she was focused on generosity, service, and loving relationships, but she got all of that earthly stuff. If you focus on the earthly, such as money, recognition, and power, you're never going to get to significance. But if you focus on significance, you'll be amazed at how much success can come your way.

Wright

I spoke with Truett Cathy recently and was impressed by what a down to earth good man he seems to be. When you started talking about him closing on Sunday, all of my friends—when they found out that I had talked to him—said, "Boy, he must be a great Christian man, but he's rich and all this." I said, "Well, to put his faith into perspective—by closing on Sunday—it cost him $500 million a year." He lives his faith, doesn't he?

Blanchard

Absolutely, but he still outsells everybody else.

Wright

That's right.

Blanchard

They were recently chosen the number one quick service restaurant in Los Angeles. They only have five restaurants here and they've only been here for a year.

Wright

The simplest market scheme, I told him, tripped me up. I walked by his first Chick-fil-A I had ever seen, and some girl came out with chicken stuck on toothpicks and handed me one; I just grabbed it and ate it, it's history from there on.

Blanchard

Yes, I think so. It's really special. It is so important that people understand generosity, service, and loving relationships because too many people are running around like a bunch of peacocks. You even see pastors, who say, how many in your congregation; authors, how many books have you sold? Business, what's your profit margin? What's your sales? The reality is that's all well and good, but I think what you need to focus on is the other. I think if business did that more and we got Wall Street off our backs with all the short term evaluation, we'd be a lot better off.

Wright

Absolutely. There seems to be a clear theme that winds through many of your books that have to do with success in business and organizations that is how people are treated by management and how they feel about their value to a company. Is this an accurate observation? If so, can you elaborate on it?

Blanchard

Yes, it's a very accurate observation. See, I think the profit is the applause you get for taking care of your customers and creating a motivating environment for your people. Very often people think that business is only about your bottom line. But no, that happens to be the result of creating raving fan customers, which I've described with Sheldon Bowles in our book, *Raving Fans*. Customers want to brag about you, if you create an environment where people can be gung-ho and committed. You've got to take care of your customers and your people, and then your cash register is going to go ka-ching, and you can make some big bucks.

Wright

I noticed that your professional title with the Ken Blanchard Companies is somewhat unique, Chairman and Chief Spiritual Officer. What does your title mean to you personally and to your company? How does it affect the books you choose to write?

Blanchard

I remember having lunch with Max DuPree one time, the legendary Chairman of Herman Miller, who wrote a wonderful book called *Leadership Is An Art.* I said, "What's your job?" He said, "I basically work in the vision area." And I said, "Well, what do you do?" He said, "I'm like a third grade teacher. I say our vision and values over, and over, and over again until people get it right, right, right." I decided from that, I was going to become the Chief Spiritual Officer, which means I would be working in the vision, values, and energy part of our business. I ended up leaving a morning message every day for everybody in our company. (We have about 275 to 300 around the country, in Canada, and the U.K. Then we have partners in about thirty nations.)

I leave a voice mail every morning, and I do three things with that as Chief Spiritual Officer. One, people tell me who we need to pray for. Two, people tell me who we need to praise—our unsung heroes and people like that. And then three, I leave an inspirational morning message. I really am kind of the cheerleader, the energy bunny in our company, and the reminder of why we're here and what we're trying to do. We think that our business in the Ken Blanchard Companies is to help people to lead at a higher level, help individuals and organizations. Our mission statement is to unleash the power and potential of people and organizations for the common good. So if we are going to do that, we've really got to believe in that. I'm working on getting more Chief Spiritual Officers around the country. I think it's a great title and we should get more of them.

Wright

So those people for whom you pray, where do you get the names?

Blanchard

The people in the company tell me who needs help, whether it's a spouse who is sick, or kids who are sick, or they are worried about something. We've got over five years of data about the power of prayer, which is pretty important. Like this morning, my inspirational message was, my wife and five members of our company walked sixty miles last weekend, twenty miles a day for three days, to raise money for breast cancer research. It was amazing. I went down and waved them all in as they came. They had a ceremony, and they raised 7.6 million dollars. There were over three thousand people walking, and a lot of the walkers were dressed in pink; they were cancer victors, people who had overcome it. There were even men walking with pictures of their wives who had died from breast cancer. I thought it was incredible. There wasn't one mention in the major San Diego papers on Monday. I said, "Isn't that just something."

We have to be an island of positive influence because all you see in the paper today is about Michael Jackson and Scott Peterson and Kobe Bryant and this kind of thing, and here you get all these thousands of people out there walking and trying to make a difference, and nobody thinks it's news. So every morning I pump people up about what life's about, about what's going on. That's what my Chief Spiritual Officer is about.

Wright

I had the pleasure of reading one of your current releases, *The Leadership Pill*.

Blanchard

Yes.

Wright

I must admit that my first thought was how short the book was. I wondered if I was going to get my money's worth, which by the way, I most certainly did. Many of your books are brief and based on a fictitious story. Most business books in the market today are hundreds of pages in length and are read almost like a textbook. Will you talk a little bit about why you write these short books, and about the premise of *The Leadership Pill?*

Blanchard

My relationship with Spencer Johnson developed when we wrote *The One Minute Manager*. As you know he wrote *Who Moved My Cheese*, which was a phenomenal success. He wrote children's books, and I was a storyteller. You know Jesus taught using parables. My favorite books were, *Jonathan Livingston Seagull* and *The Little Prince,* and *Og Mandino* is the greatest of them all. They are all great parables. I started writing parables because people can get into the story and learn the contents of the story, and they don't bring their judgmental hats into reading. You write a regular book and they'll say, "Well, where did you get the research?" They get into that judgmental side. Our books get them emotionally involved and they learn. *The Leadership Pill* is a fun story about a pharmaceutical company who thinks that they have discovered the secret to leadership, and they can put the ingredients in a pill. When they announce it, the country goes crazy because everybody knows we need more effective leaders. When they release it, it outsells Viagra. The founders of the company start selling off stock and they call them Pillionaires. But along comes this guy who calls himself "the effective manager," and he challenges them to a no-pill challenge. If they identify two non-performing groups, he'll take on one and let somebody on the pill take another one, and he guarantees he will out-perform by the end of the year. They agree, but of course, they give him a drug test every week to make sure he's not sneaking pills on the side.

I wrote the book with Marc Muchnick, who is a young guy in his early thirties. We did a major study of what this interesting "Y" generation, the young people of today, want from leaders, and this is a secret blend that this effective manager uses. When you think about it, David, it is really powerful on terms of what people want from a leader.

Number one, they want integrity. A lot of people have talked about that in the past, but these young people will walk if they see people say one thing and do another. A lot of us walk to the bathroom and out into the halls to talk about it. But these people will quit. They don't want somebody to say something and not do it. The second thing they want is a partnership relationship. They hate superior/subordinate. I mean, what awful terms those are. You know: the "head" of the department and the hired "hands"—you don't even give them a head. "What do you do? I'm in supervision. I see things a lot clearer than these stupid idiots." They want to be treated as partners. If they can get a financial partnership, great. If they can't, they really want a minimum of psychological partnership where they can bring their brains to work and make decisions. Then finally, they want affirmation. They not only want to be caught doing things right, but they want to be affirmed for who they are. They want to be known as a person, not as a number.

So those are the three ingredients that this effective manager uses. They are wonderful values if you think about them.

Rank-order values for any organization is number one: integrity. In our company we call it ethics. It is our number one value. The number two value is partnership. In our company we call it relationships. Number three is affirmation, which is being affirmed as a human being. I think that ties into relationships, too. They are wonderful values that can drive behavior in a great way.

Wright

I believe most people in today's business culture would agree that success in business has everything to do with successful leadership. In *The Leadership Pill*, you present a simple but profound premise, that leadership is not something you do to people. It's something you do with them. At face value, that seems incredibly obvious. But you must have found in your research and observations that leaders in today's culture do not get this. Would you speak to that issue?

Blanchard

Yes, and I think what often happens in this is the human ego. There are too many leaders out there who are self-serving. They're not serving leaders. They think the sheep are there for the benefit of the shepherd. All the power, money, fame and recognition moves up the hierarchy, and they forget that the real action in business is not up the hierarchy—it's in the one to one moment-to-moment interactions that your front line people have with your customers. It's how the phone is answered. It's how problems are dealt with and those kinds of things. If you don't think that you're doing leadership with them, rather you're doing it to them, after a while they won't take care of your customers. I was at a store recently, not Nordstrom's, where I normally would go, and I thought of something I had to share with my wife, Margie. I asked the guy behind the counter in Men's Wear, "Can I use your phone?" He said, "No!" I said, "You're kidding me. I can always use the phone at Nordstrom's." He said, "Look, buddy, they won't let *me* use the phone here. Why should I let you use the phone?" That is an example of leadership that's done to them not with them. People want a partnership. People want to be involved in a way that really makes a difference.

Wright

Dr. Blanchard, the time has flown by and there are so many more questions I'd like to ask you. In closing, would you mind sharing with our readers some thoughts on success? If you were mentoring a small group of men and women, and one of their central goals was to become successful, what kind of advice would you give them?

Blanchard

Well, I would first of all say, "What are you focused on?" I think if you are focused on success as being, as I said earlier, accumulation of money, recognition, power, or status, I think you've got the wrong target. I think what you need to really be focused on is how can you be generous in the use of your time and your talent and your treasure and touch. How can you serve people rather than be served? How can you develop caring, loving relationships with people? My sense is if you will focus on those things, success in the traditional sense will come to you. But if you go out and say, "Man, I'm going to make a fortune, and I'm going to do this," and those kinds of things, you might even get some of those numbers. I think you do become an adult when you realize that you are here to give rather than to get. You're here to serve not to be served. I would just say to people, "Life is such a very special occasion. Don't miss it by aiming at a target that bypasses other people, because we're really here to serve each other." So that's what I would share with people.

Wright

Well, what an enlightening conversation, Dr. Blanchard. I really want you to know how much I appreciate all this time you've taken with me for this interview. I know that our readers will learn from this, and I really appreciate you being with us today.

Blanchard

Well, thank you so much, David. I really enjoyed my time with you. You've asked some great questions that made me think, but I hope are helpful to other people because as I say, life is a special occasion.

Wright

Today we have been talking with Dr. Ken Blanchard. He is the author of the phenomenal best selling book, *The One Minute Manager.* Also, the fact that he's the Chief Spiritual Officer of his company should make us all think about how we are leading our companies and leading our families and leading anything, whether it is in church or civic organizations. I know I will.

Thank you so much, Dr. Blanchard, for being with us today on *Getting Things Done.*

Blanchard

Good to be with you, David.

About The Author

Few people have created more of a positive impact on the day-to-day management of people and companies than Dr. Kenneth Blanchard, who is known around the world simply as "Ken."

When Ken speaks, he speaks from the heart with warmth and humor. His unique gift is to speak to an audience and communicate with each individual as if they were alone and talking one on one. He is a polished storyteller with a knack for making the seemingly complex easy to understand.

Ken has been a guest on a number of national television programs, including Good Morning America and The Today Show, and has been featured in *Time, People, U.S. News & World Report,* and a host of other popular publications.

He earned his bachelor's degree in government and philosophy from Cornell University, his master's degree in sociology and counseling from Colgate University, and his PhD in educational administration and leadership from Cornell University.

Dr. Ken Blanchard
The Ken Blanchard Companies
125 State Place
Escondido, California 92029
Phone: 800-728-6000
Fax: 760-489-8407
www.kenblanchard.com

Chapter 3

JEAN MALE

THE INTERVIEW

David Wright (Wright)

I'm delighted that Jean (Mowrey) Male has accepted our invitation to speak with us today because she has a long-standing reputation for getting things done. When it comes to making things happen Jean quotes the saying, "Experience is the name we have given our mistakes." She will share a bit of what she learned (sometimes painfully) as she broke worldwide records in business development, launched and managed multimillion dollar pharmaceutical products and drug devices, hired and developed award-winning teams, and served as President of the pharmaceutical industry's training association.

Jean has been published and interviewed by more than twenty journals on sales, performance improvement, training, and management topics. She is a highly sought-after keynote speaker of tremendous substance on topics to improve individual and organizational performance.

Since 1997, Ms. Male has served as CEO of Emp-Higher Performance Development, Inc., a firm specializing in training, motivational speaking, and performance consulting where she has authored a content powerhouse of more than thirty proven training programs.

Ms. Male, welcome to *Getting Things Done.*

Jean Male

Thank you, David.

Wright

Let me start by asking, when you think about getting things done, what does that mean to you?

Male

Getting things done isn't just about checking items off a checklist. Getting things done is about getting ahead *and* getting a life—two important objectives that appear diametrically opposed to many of us. When was the last time you said, "I don't have enough time"?

William Penn understood well when he said, "Time is what we want most and use worst." I regularly convict myself of this truism. If we think of time as a loan and ourselves as loan officers we are forced to calculate a likely return on how the time is invested for the greatest return. We've all heard the saying, "time is money," yet we are far more cavalier about spending time than spending money.

It's impossible to cover getting things done without acknowledging that time is our most valuable resource—more than money. The idea of time management is a misnomer because we cannot manage time. We can only manage ourselves. We can always find ways to get or make more money but time is the great equalizer. We have the same amount of time to use each day as Donald Trump. It's how we use it that counts. Because no matter how smart, talented, or lucky we are we cannot squeeze more than twenty-four hours out of every day. Unlike money, we cannot save or manage it. It falls away moment by moment and is forever gone.

Think About It . . .

Why is it that pulling a fifty dollar bill out of our wallets creates automatic discernment about the value we are getting for it, yet we fritter away time.

This isn't to suggest that we should hyper-focus on getting things done every waking minute. The goal is to create positive intention around how we spend our most precious commodity regardless of whether we are doing, delegating, or relaxing.

Wright

How do you suggest our readers get the highest return on their time and enable them to get things done?

Male

There are five areas that allow us to get things done and get a life. They are: create alignment and clarity, discipline your mind, slay the dinosaur ego, create stability, and hone interpersonal skills. Because the first four topics may be common sense but not common practice, I'll pose some questions to serve as a reality check of what we know versus what we do. Then, for the fifth topic, I'll give some personal inventory tools for getting things done.

Wright

Excellent! To start with the first of the five areas, will you define what you mean by create alignment and clarity?

Male

In part we are better at discerning value when it comes to spending money because we typically get a tangible return or some instant gratification, whereas we often don't when spending increments of time that may ultimately yield better health, advanced education, and well adjusted children.

To get a sense of satisfaction on time investments that won't pay off right away we need a clear vision of what we are working toward. We may be so overwhelmed by goals and objectives at work that we don't want to think about them when it comes to our careers or personal lives. We tend to belong to at least one of three different camps:

1. No written goals (fear of failure or success)
2. Too many or unrealistic goals (more like a wish list)
3. Vague goals (no plan to get there)

So it's hard to discern value and get a return on our time investments if our goals are not aligned with what we want, need, and value. This is no easy task because we may say we value health, family, and spiritual aspects but spend all of our time on tasks that don't align with those values. Worse still, how much time is spent daily that doesn't even accomplish our work goals for the paycheck to get what we want, need, and value? Aligning one's goals with what one truly values creates the synergy and passion to get things done. A program called, "Your Lot in Life . . . Choosing to Park or Build on It" helps to create goals with alignment to priorities and balance. Think about these questions:

- Which of the three "goals camps" best describes me?
- Do I have short- and long-term work and personal goals?
- How much of my day is spent accomplishing tasks unrelated to goals?
- What do I want my legacy to be? What will they say about me at my funeral?
- Are my goals and daily tasks aligned with what I truly want, need, and value?

Wright

How do you suggest we condition ourselves to discipline the mind?

Male

The barrage and pace of information called the Information Age might be more aptly called the Age of Distraction where each of us has a sense of what it is to suffer from attention deficit disorder. When we reflect on why we don't accomplish what we aim to each day or week, the answer is often found in a lack of focus on goals while attending to voicemail, e-mail, hard copy correspondence, drop-in visits, long meetings, phone calls, and other distractions. At work or at home most of us have a task list, but to get things done we need to make sure the lists are helping us rather than distracting us. We should ask ourselves questions such as:

- "Are the items on my list aligned with my short- and long-term goals?
- Does this list consist of both the most important and urgent things?
- Throughout the day (awaken from your tasks trance) ask yourself, "Is what I'm doing, or about to do, getting me closer to accomplishing my goals?"
- Ask yourself (while scratching items from your "to do" list), "Are things being done as well as they can be or only as well as they should be done?

The ability to discipline the mind is about more than time and list management. Productivity has a lot to do with awareness of one's thoughts and the power that our state of mind has on our productivity and quality of life. This includes clearly envisioning success as well as developing the ability to identify and replace frivolous thoughts and worry. Athletes, prisoners of war, and now modern medicine have acknowledged the power of prayer and positive thinking. We do well to understand and harness the metaphysical concept that thoughts are things. Our minds can literally create success and good health or the opposite, so it's vital that we control our thoughts rather than allowing them to control us. These concepts are also well known by the likes of Dale Carnegie and Zen monks and have been scientifically validated. The ability to control one's thoughts and focus on goals with positive intention is vital to getting things done and getting a life.

Wright

Your third topic area, slay the dinosaur ego, seems like a unique approach to getting things done. Can you tell us a little more about that?

Male

Statements like, "That's the way I've always done it," or "I've always been successful doing—" are frequently uttered by the human dinosaur. It may be expedient to do things as we've always done them but standing still in the tar pit is setting oneself up for extinction. Peter Drucker put it another way when he said, "If you haven't acquired a new idea or abandoned an old one in the last quarter, you are on your way to becoming obsolete and unmarketable."

Sadly, there is an inherent resistance to raising the bar for adults. Adults can be very resistant to trying something new because of the discomfort of incompetence and fear of looking foolish. In training, this manifests in veteran sales reps who think they are above training or role-play. This prima donna attitude is ruinous to innovation and coaching. Many companies pander to the egos of tenured employees unwittingly encourage them to stagnate. Those who resist growing pains because they think they've "arrived" are intellectually expired or dead.

Creating a belief system or being part of a culture that demands and rewards intellectual curiosity and innovation is key. This belief system and culture celebrates mistakes, lessons learned, and progress toward not just getting things done, but finding new ways to get things done better, faster, or safer. Until we slay the dinosaur ego that resists doing things differently, we will soon be of limited use, if not a true impediment, to our employers and ourselves. Some questions to stimulate thought in this area are:

- When was the last time you resisted trying something new?
- What were you afraid of: looking bad, getting lost, failing?
- What was the worst thing that probably would have happened if you tried?
- What was the best thing that might have happened if you tried?
- What should you seriously consider doing differently soon?

Wright

You talk about creating stability. How does this play a valuable part in getting things done?

Male

Our work time and goals are often spelled out for us, so our biggest challenge can be the need to create boundaries and balance. What pays the bills and what gives us a sense of purpose can sometimes be at cross-purposes because we want the American dream— yep, we want it all! Do we want prestige and promotion but feel victimized by our inability to spend enough time with family?

This takes us back to having a clear sense of what we want, need, and value. Most of us don't spend as much time planning the direction of our lives as we do planning a vacation. Failing to plan and work toward what we want to be when we grow up and grow old means that life happens as though we are a leaf buffeted about by the wind.

In order to create stability, consider questions such as:
- What do you value most? Rank in order of importance to what you value, want, and need:
    1. Recognition (promotion, awards)
    2. Service (make things better, helping)
    3. Material things (money and goods)
    4. Belonging (family, spiritual affiliations, work)
    5. Self-actualization (learning, accomplishment)
    6. Health (fitness, vitality, looks)
    7. Mission (a cause, an organization or religion)
- Have you been brutally honest with yourself about what you really want, need, and value?
- Do you have clarity around what you are willing to do as well as what you are willing to give up?
- Do you have a roadmap or plan?

1. In the past year, how much time have you spent planning or preparing for a vacation or holidays?
2. Compare your answer to the above question with how much time you spent charting your future, goal planning, or retirement.

Creating stability means being true to oneself. There is no universal right or wrong, there is only what each of us needs to find meaning and balance; whether it's relationships with family and friends, a focus on health or spirit, pursuit of self-actualization, hobbies, or service.

Lack of focused balance creates enormous stress, feelings of inadequacy, and the oft-accompanying depression so many suffer from today. Naturally the scales of responsibility will tip in one direction but they can't stay out of kilter too long without becoming a stifling trap. The accolades from a great work ethic can fuel workaholism. As a recovering workaholic I've seen how easily the rewards can distract us from ourselves and our lives. Workaholics are at risk for poor health, disappointed children, divorce, depression, and loneliness.

Getting things done and getting a life doesn't happen by accident. It requires honesty, clarity, the creation of boundaries, and gives us permission to be honest about what we are and are not willing to do or sacrifice to be true to ourselves. Then once clear, it is a purposeful pursuit of activities according to those goals and values. Clear intention around what we aim to do and become helps create focus. It means the difference between getting things done or getting the right (or meaningful) things done.

Wright

You mentioned earlier that these four topic areas will help you do a necessary reality check. Will you tell us about the fifth area that you refer to as a personal inventory for success?

Male

The first four topics highlight inward focused tactics that may be more common sense than common practice. The last one, Interpersonal Skills, is outward focused. In fact, even if we don't do the first four, this one can help us succeed in spite of ourselves.

It's interesting to note that much of Ken Blanchard's comments in the previous interview highlight the importance of people skills for effective leadership. He mentions "The Leadership Pill" about a pharmaceutical company that discovered the secret to leadership and put it in a pill but found out that there's no shortcut to effective leadership. This isn't exclusive to leadership. Getting things done involves all aspects of working well with others.

Relationships are actually more important to getting things done in today's fast-paced and sometimes impersonal Information Age. Because we must often rely on others to accomplish our goals it's important to know how to enroll them in our cause. One of the most pivotal lessons is understanding that when all things are equal (e.g. job offer, products or price), people want to work with, and buy from, those they *know, like, trust,* and *respect.*

Some personal things to thing about are:

- Consider your last major purchase, job offer/job candidates, or supplier choice. How much did one or all of the *know-like-trust-respect* factors impact your choice?
- Think of a situation where others need to choose you or your services over others. Ask yourself, "How do I stack up in each aspect of the *know, like, trust, respect* factors?"

Wright

That is very interesting. Will you give our readers some tips on shoring up opportunities in these areas?

Male

The *know, like, trust, respect* continuum is about moving from creating rapport to establishing a true relationship. A fundamental, yet underestimated aspect of "know" is making it our business to learn and remember names. This continues to be an important challenge for me, which is compounded by exposure to so many people while speaking and training. But beyond those circumstances, how often is it that we encounter the same people in business, social interactions, spiritual, or professional organizations for years, yet upon seeing them, nod an uncomfortable familiarity because we don't know or remember their names? Regardless of circumstance it creates and invisible barrier because it appears that we didn't care enough to learn and remember their names.

Conversely, when people remember our name and are happy to see us the barrier vaporizes. It makes them more memorable and gives us a reason to remember and use their name. Until we can say someone's name upon seeing him or her, we aren't even at the "know"—the beginning of rapport—of the relationship continuum. The key to getting things done in business is that this works both ways.

Rapport to Relationship Continuum

Know   Like   Trust   Respect

Another way to increase your "know" equity is to network. While it's been said that "your network is net worth," you don't need to be a networking workhorse! It's not about knowing everyone who's someone; it's about knowing just enough people that one of your contacts is likely to know a tried and true resource to help you "get it done." Think about these questions:

- Whose name should you make a point to learn and remember?
- What organization(s) should you join or regularly attend to expand your network?

Wright

How does the like aspect of the relationship continuum impact our ability to get things done?

Male

The number one way to get things done is to be likeable. In my early career as a Training Director in a Fortune 500 company, I equated being liked with the back-slapping, glad-handing, good ole boy network that I regarded with disdain. I believed that it was only important to get results and be good at my job. My philosophy was that I wasn't in a popularity contest; I had an international reputation for making things happen so I frankly didn't care whether people liked me. I truly believed that respect was the key to success . . . and I was dead wrong. My subsequent success was much harder than it ever needed to be. Right or wrong, I learned that being likeable is the *single* greatest career maker or breaker!

The reason the "Peter Principle" (people rising to the level of their incompetence) exists is because someone promoted them because they liked them more than others who were more qualified. Often these are buddies who get brought in to a new company because the hiring manager likes and trusts the person and knows their friend "has their back." In the end, likeability and trust wins the day and the deal.

Today's workforce is no longer loyal to corporations but individual employees are loyal to their line managers. This fact is borne out by exit interviews and numerous surveys documenting that the number one reason people leave or stay with a company is due to their direct manager. If you've ever been in sales you know that you would be willing to go the extra mile or make extra calls each day to help your boss even if your personal sales were above quota.

Conversely, those who don't like their manager lack motivation to expand discretionary effort to help the manager by doing anything beyond what is required. Managers who are likeable are doing what is called, "Managing the White Space." It's a common issue seen in our performance consulting practice and in everyday life. We tend to enroll others in our cause more by being likeable than by using authority. Ask yourself:

- How likeable are you . . . really?
- Do people's faces light up because they seem genuinely happy to see you?

How many times have you seen people with the right idea that would fix a real problem who will never "get it done" because they unwittingly alienate rather than motivate others to their cause? A lot of tension arises from being unaware that our own style may alienate those with different styles.

A loose analogy might be how a person from New York City and someone from the Deep South might feel an immediate disconnection or tension simply because their communication style and pace differ. It's well known that managers hire in their own image, which only means that we tend to like people who are like us. Right or wrong, to get things done through others is to appreciate the fact that personality or behavioral styles are the ultimate diversity to unite or divide us.

Behavioral styles impact all aspects of business, selling, family, and social relationships. Knowing how to identify and adapt to others is a major aspect of influence to create positive and productive interactions.

Think About It . . .
- Whom do you feel most comfortable and least comfortable interacting with on the job?
- How much is this person's style more or less like yours?

- How does his or her style help or hinder whether you want to know, whether you like, trust, or respect him or her?

Pivotal to getting things done is developing a deep understanding of how behavioral style impacts relationships and how relationships impact success. At the very least, adapting to styles helps us "play nicely in the sandbox" without inadvertently kicking sand into another's eyes.

Wright

How do styles impact our ability to get things done?

Male

Every day we see the following behaviors in business meetings:
1. Someone going off on tangents, interrupting, and monopolizing discussion.
2. Another watching time, interrupting and saying, "Here's what we need to do."
3. A person being steamrolled while quietly wishing someone would ask what he or she thinks or feels.
4. Those who rigidly adhere to the agenda, demand proof, creating protocols and procedures.

Wright

That scenario sounds like what goes on in many meetings. Are there names for the styles or meeting behaviors?

Male

The four styles exhibited by the meeting behaviors described were: (1) Charisma, (2) Control, (3) Caring, and (4) Correct.

Wright

What resources and examples can you provide to help our readers identify styles and their impact on getting things done?

Male

I'll provide Emp-Higher's Behavioral Styles chart for readers to reference as I provide examples:

Working with Behavioral Styles

Behavior Traits	Control	Charisma	Caring	Correct
Pace/Focus	Fast/Results	Fast/People	Slow/Team	Slow/Task
Prefers to be	In Charge	Admired	Liked	Accurate
Likes you to be	To the Point	Stimulating	Pleasant	Conscien-tious
Key wants	Results Productivity	Recognition Applause	Compatibility Security	Precision Accuracy
Irritated by	Inefficiency Indecision	Boredom Routine	Insensitivity Impatience	Surprises Unpredict-ability
Disagreement Is seen as	Competition	Inflexible	Rude	To be avoided
Decision Making is	Decisive	Spontaneous	Considered	Deliberate

A fundamental example is that people may automatically disrespect others whose pace or way of processing information differs from theirs. Consider how the Control style might clash with the Caring style on a team project.

Refer to the Working with Behavioral Styles chart as you consider:

- The Control style demands that the Correct style deliver information quickly and succinctly.
- The Correct style values accuracy and cannot bear being wrong. The Control's interruptions and refusal to let them give the right information is frustrating to the Correct style.
- The Control style becomes increasingly agitated by what they deem a maddening amount of detail and demand that the Correct style "cut to the chase."
- The Correct style disengages because they want no part of inadequate (read "incorrect") information on which to base decisions.
- The Control style can't stand the "analysis paralysis" and the Correct style can't abide by snap decisions without adequate data or full risk/benefit analyses.

Lack of style adaptation often creates frustration, lack of respect, and prevents us from getting things done through others. If we could read the minds of both individuals during the interaction, the only thought they might have in common is, "You don't get me . . . I don't like you."

Differing styles will surely clash but can you imagine a decision being made by a task force of all one style? Conversely, decisions are far better and task forces more productive when all four styles are involved and respected. Only then can we provide good feelings and solutions to problems.

Imagine the Charisma and Correct scenario if one were trying to be hired or selling to the other.

Wright

What can our readers do to apply behavioral styles to being more likeable and getting things done through others?

Male

The takeaway is that the person with the goal or agenda should identify and adapt to the other person's syle. Only when we adapt to the styles of others can we minimize tension and present our ideas in a way that gives others the "ears to hear" our ideas or message. It's a simple appreciation of "it's not what we say, but how we say it" or how to adjust our approach, pace, and word choices.

Regardless of whether we are in a position of authority or not, the ability to adapt dramatically impacts influence. Some questions to think about are:

- Bring to mind a subject, idea, or proposal that you need to gain approval for.
- Who is the person who can say yes or influence the approval?
- By reviewing the Behavioral Styles Chart, which style do you think that person exhibits?
- Review the table to sketch out how you might present the idea in a way that will give that person the "eyes to see" and the "ears to hear" the value of your idea by tapping in to what he or she wants, needs, and values.

Wright

Will you give us your definition of trust and how we can apply that to help us get things done?

Male

Living and working in ways that consistently demonstrate ethics and integrity.

Consider the movie, *Saving Private Ryan*, where Tom Hanks, playing the sergeant, inwardly agrees but refuses to acknowledge his troop's assessment that their mission is "FUBARed." I'll replace the first two words with "Foolish and Unrealistic." The rest of the acronym stands for "Beyond Any/All Recognition." It's an excellent example of how bad-mouthing—regardless of justification—is one of the fastest ways to destroy morale and lose trust and respect. To be sure, the bad-mouther is a hero of the disgruntled and a promotional pariah to management. Regardless of talent or accomplishments, it's career suicide.

If the situation is unbearable, it's best to grin and bear it while planning an exit strategy than to undermine management or worse still, to quit and stay. It's difficult to get things done if we've painted ourselves into a corner. Trust is created over time by what we do as much as what we refrain from doing.

- How do most people look upon the person who bemoans policies or berates management—even if they agree with the bad-mouther?
- Can your company trust you to do your job with integrity and loyalty even when you disagree with a policy, direction, or new mandate?
- On a scale of one to ten, how much do your co-workers and management really trust you to cover their back, give them credit, keep a confidence, or support their decisions?
- Do you always do what you say you will, when you say you will?

Wright

The last great differentiator you mentioned was respect. Please let our readers know how this can play an important part in the process.

Male

Achieving greatness is not a shortcut to respect. Those who have accomplished much must "get over themselves" if they want to achieve their true potential. Sure, a lofty title or resume may afford some degree of automatic respect but respect is a highly reciprocal proposition. Consider how little we truly respect those who surround themselves with "yes" men and women. Those who are enamored of themselves, their ideas, or accomplishments are rarely granted true respect, especially if they fail to value the contributions, differences, and opinions of others. Acting otherwise is interpreted as arrogance that's unforgivable. This holds true whether we are right or wrong and even under dire circumstances as evidenced by the backlash against the U.S. for not gaining consensus before declaring war on Iraq.

Part of earning respect requires an attitude of, *"None of us is as smart as all of us,"* and is one of the secrets to getting things done (and often better) through others. Ask yourself these questions:

- Do you take yourself or your job too seriously?
- Do people consider you open, authentic, and approachable?
- Do you actively seek to understand different viewpoints?
- Do you invite honest discussion around the good, bad, and ugly aspects of key issues?

Wright

You have given us much to think about.

Male

I appreciate that perfect, 24/7 execution of what I've suggested is a tall order. I sincerely believe that if readers just focus on the one or two topics that resonate, they will find getting things done a lot more pleasant and productive.

Wright

Thank you for openly sharing some lessons learned and many valuable insights.

Male

Thank you for inviting me to speak. It's been a pleasure.

About the Author

JEAN (MOWREY) MALE brings more than two decades of lessons from the trenches in pharmaceutical sales, marketing, management, business development, and training. Ms. Male has been extensively published and interview by major sales, management and training magazines, broken worldwide sales records launched and managed multimillion-dollar pharmaceutical product portfolios, and hired and developed award-winning teams, groomed fourteen reports for management, and authored more than thirty proven training programs. For the past decade, Ms. Male has been President and CEO of Emp-Higher Performance Development, Inc., New Jersey based firm specializing in training, motivational speaking, and performance consulting.

She is a highly sought-after keynote speaker of that clients have nick-named "The Velvet Hammer" for her ability to nail the needs of the audience and drive even difficult points home with finesse.

Ms. Male is a past President of the SPBT (Society of Pharmaceutical and is an honorary Commander in the United States Air Force and Biotech Trainers), formerly the NSPST. Jean holds professional memberships in the ISPI (International Society for Performance Improvement), ASTD (American Society for Training and Development), HBA (Healthcare Businesswomen's Association) and the NSA (National Speakers Association).

Jean (Mowrey) Male
Phone: 856.787.1107 ext.111
Fax: 856.787.1108
E-mail: jeanmale@emphigher.com
www.emphigher.com

Chapter 4

RICK HOUCEK

David Wright (Wright)

Today we're talking with Rick Houcek. Rick's singular company purpose is: *to provide high-octane, world-class strategic planning systems for business and life*, helping Top Gun leaders, teams, and individuals to succeed "on purpose, most of the time," rather than "by accident, some of the time." He does this in five primary ways: (1) facilitating his *Power Planning*™ strategic planning retreats for small and mid-size companies, (2) licensing the use of his Power Planning system to other consultants, coaches, and trainers, (3) leading his *Passion Planning*™ workshops for ambitious individuals on self-motivation, personal life planning, and goal-setting, (4) delivering high-energy motivational keynotes, and (5) one-on-one success coaching.

He has coached entrepreneurs, CEOs, presidents, and senior executives for over ten years, and is former president of Ross Roy Advertising, an Atlanta ad agency and division of the $700 million Ross Roy Group. A University of Missouri graduate, he is a member of the

National Speakers Association and has been recognized in *Who's Who Among U.S. Executives* and *Who's Who in Georgia.*

Rick is married and passionately devoted to his soul mate, Robbie, and he adores his awesome grown twins, Val and Chip. He has four fanatical life passions: his family, his personal health and fitness, helping others prosper through his business and friendships, and playing competitive baseball on a traveling men's team.

Rick, welcome to *Getting Things Done: Keys to a Successful Business.*

Rick Houcek (Houcek)

Thank you, David, it's my honor to be here.

Wright

Rick, let's get right to it. You've gone on record as saying that businesses today are *not* suffering from a shortage of good ideas . . . yet for some reason, many are still not prospering. Help us understand this.

Houcek

That's true, many are not prospering. The statistics are staggering. In the United States about half of new companies are out of business by the five-year point, about 80 percent are gone by the ten-year point, and it gets worse from there. That's a frightening failure rate. It begs the question: *what is it about sustaining positive results that is so difficult to master in running a business?*

Even for those who survive longer, many are not prospering to the level they *could*. They're leaving volume and profits on the table for a competitor to get. Why? The answer is largely the same in all companies. To explain it, let me start at the beginning.

I have yet to find, work with, or read about a company that is suffering from lousy, unworkable, or too *few* ideas to *grow the business profitably*. Great ideas are *everywhere* in the organization. Certainly leaders at the very top—chairmen, CEOs, presidents, and entrepreneurs—are always thinking about growth . . . new markets to enter, new products and services to introduce, new geographies to expand into, new customers to pursue, getting more business from current customers, and more. Second tier management is also charged with growth responsibilities, whether it's getting more sales from existing customers, or finding new ones. Middle managers and below are probably more concerned with tactical "inward" issues than strategic "outward" opportunities, but nonetheless, their heads are jammed with helpful ideas too—more operationally focused—like how to improve or speed up internal processes, how to fix a broken system or create a better one, how to prevent or solve turf wars between internal departments, and so on.

I'm constantly asking company employees, at *all* levels: *what's the single most important thing you feel this company could do to improve sales and profits?* When I ask, up and down the line, in all positions, in every company, to every person I've asked this question, they *always* have an answer. Their ideas are often different, but always plentiful. After they tell me, I ask: *And what could you do to make that happen?*

They always have an answer to *that*, too—I so seldom hear *I don't know.* My next question is: *what happened when you did it?* This is where it gets puzzling because too often the answer is: *well, I haven't done it yet.* Further probing reveals they haven't even told anyone of the problem or opportunity, let alone their solution. There are several reasons why: they think no one will listen, they're afraid of being wrong, they've been shot down before, or they feel someone in top leadership should come to them and ask.

Wright

So you're saying the ideas exist, but aren't coming forward?

Houcek

Exactly. But it's even worse than that. Just as often, I hear they brought the idea forward, it was discussed, maybe even started, but it died on the vine for lack of interest or inability to execute.

There is one key trait that unifies all high-achieving people and is shared by all successful companies as well: *they take action—massive action.* They don't just talk, they *do.* They are *relentless implementers.* They get it done and take no prisoners.

People and companies that fail to grasp this are doomed to frustrating, repetitive failure. And their ultimate fate, one day, will be to join the staggering statistics of "out-of-business" companies. Oh sure, they'll win once in a while, more by accident than intention when luck intervenes in their favor. But that's no big thing. Anyone can succeed that way—occasionally, with no effort. Even a last place team will win *some* games. In fact, there are many companies that win just often enough to keep the doors open, limping along from one occasional victory to another. Those leaders are not building vibrant, growing, electric organizations—they're barely getting by, losing steam by the minute, in danger of one day not making payroll.

To be truly successful and earn continued positive results, it requires not winning only every so often, but winning on a sustained, repeated basis. Vince Lombardi said it best: "Winning is not a *some*-time thing. It's an all-the-time thing."

Wright

That's what is so hard to do: *sustain* results, again and again, over the long-haul.

Houcek

Yes, but ironically, it's not hard for the reason you'd think. Most would think sustaining long-term results is difficult because they are not *capable*. Low self-esteem drives them to think it can happen for others, but not for them.

Actually though, it has nothing to do with capability. In my mind, *everyone* is capable. It has everything to do with the willingness to do whatever it takes to succeed, no matter how painful, rigorous, or time-consuming. That's the margin of difference: the willingness to plow forward through all the problems, barriers, and roadblocks—no matter what. Every day you have to think of yourself as an NFL running back with twenty yards to the end zone and a brick wall of defensive giants blocking your path. Watch the best, darting in and out, zigging and zagging, hurdling over those on the ground, shoulder faking, stiff-arming tacklers, and when necessary, lowering their heads and bowling over or through a defender.

Some guys just smell the end zone and won't be denied. They don't make it every play, but they get farther than the ones who go down at first contact. That starts with attitude—a belief that your desired end result *belongs* to you and no one can take it away from you—and every step, movement, and action you take supports that belief, from the moment your eyes open in the morning until your head hits the pillow at night.

But all that *belief* and *attitude* I just described is only one step in the whole process—a very important one, but only one.

Wright

So help our readers with how they can "make the leap" from *feeling incapable* all the way to *making it happen*. What's the magic about making this transition become a reality?

Houcek

It's a key part of what I help companies do, day in and day out. I'm a huge believer in "systematizing" your business and your life in every possible area you can. The more systems you have in place to keep you from having to re-invent the wheel, to help you replicate the same actions for the same repetitive opportunities and problems, the more effective and efficient you'll be. It's a simple formula: create great systems, implement them religiously, track their performance, modify where necessary, and hold people accountable for doing so.

And by the way, many people feel strongly that you *first must believe* you can, before you really can. I used to think that too. Certainly it helps. But I've seen it happen in reverse too many times: a person with little self-esteem or self-confidence who became awesomely successful anyway. And *then* they gained their esteem and confidence and belief by virtue of that success, which was the result of taking action, plowing ahead. Let's don't kid ourselves into thinking that everyone who is successful had a boatload of self-confidence beforehand. A good many do not.

So the message is, with or without self-confidence, take action anyway.

That's where systems come into play. A critically important system I use with my business clients is a dynamic planning and implementation system I call the Power Planning™ strategic retreat. It solves—once and for all—the single biggest reason for "idea failure" in business, which is lousy implementation. That one thing—lousy implementation—kills more great ideas and broad plans than any other single factor. If you solve that, you're on your way. And I'm proud to say my Power Planning system solves it.

In fact, I've boiled it down to the most damaging reasons why implementation fails, which I call "The 9 Mortal Sins of Strategic Planning and Execution"—each of which is overcome by using my Power Planning system.

Mortal Sin #1: shooting from the hip—the lack of any kind of written plan whatsoever. This happens in a surprisingly high number of companies. I read one estimate by a government business bureau that claimed more than 80 percent of U.S. businesses have no written plan of any kind. This is frightening to me because there is so much evidence that supports the power of the written word to help us crystallize thought. A business leader whose plan resides only in his head is expecting the rest of the company's employees—who are all the enactors of the plan—to be mind readers. That's a ticket to the poorhouse.

Some leaders fear the written plan will get into the hands of competitors and other undesirables. While some elements may need to be kept confidential, the bulk of any company's plan should be shared company-wide. Expecting employees to achieve goals they aren't even aware of is ridiculous—it's irresponsible leadership.

Mortal Sin #2 is when the CEO *does* author a written strategic plan, but does so alone, and involves no one else in its creation—a tragic misstep. Buy-in to this plan can never be garnered from others who will be implementers. People don't reject their own ideas, but they'll reject the ideas of another person all day long. So closing them out of the "plan creation" process is suicidal to successful execution. Many years ago, I made this mistake as a corporate president—and I have no one but myself to blame for the sub-par results. I learned the hard way.

Wright

I would imagine those two sins alone probably account for a large majority of CEOs. But what about the leaders who *do* involve others in plan creation?

Houcek

You're right on target, and that leads me to:

Mortal Sin #3: The CEO *does* involve others in planning, but leads the planning process herself or himself. Any time the top dog calls a planning meeting, invites others to join around the table, but facilitates the meeting alone from beginning to end, is missing a key point.

No matter how objective and open the "CEO-as-facilitator" tries to be, there will be an unspoken belief by all others attending, that he or she came to the meeting with a pre-determined plan in mind and is leading the discussion in such a way as to guide everyone down the leader's intended path to create the plan he or she wanted all along, never revealing what that plan is and cleverly making them think it's *their* idea. How do I know this? Because I interview all meeting attendees before client retreats that I'm hired to facilitate and it gets uncovered there. Whenever a prior planning meeting was facilitated by the leader, that's what I hear.

I delight in asking: "So what did the CEO say when you pointed that out?" The answer is predictable: "Oh, we didn't *tell* her [or him] we felt that way. We just kept it to ourselves." In my experience, most CEOs truly did not have a pre-determined plan in mind, but it doesn't matter. Team members were convinced they did; all because the CEO facilitated the meeting.

Worse, plan execution suffers horribly because team members—who are the chief implementers of the plan they feel was cleverly jammed down their throats—are insulted and resent it. And the CEO, who left the meeting interpreting the nodding heads as acceptance and buy-in, was shocked later when implementation stunk and the plan eventually died. That's usually when I hear a CEO denounce strategic planning altogether and claim it just doesn't work. Wrong. *It works*, but only when a particular collection of critical elements are brought together, and none left out.

Mortal Sin #4 is when written goals are weak, fuzzy, and lack laser-beam clarity. Most people, despite their best efforts, write terrible goals. A goal like "Increase sales" is ridiculous, unclear, and non-motivating. Not that it's a bad idea to increase sales—of course it's not—but let's get something on paper that articulates a clear end result, has specific urgency, and gets hearts pounding.

President Kennedy's announced intention in the early '60s to *"land a man on the moon and return him safely to earth by the end of the decade"* had all the attributes of a well-crafted goal and it mobilized an entire space movement. It's worth it to write, re-write, polish, and re-polish goals until they sing with clarity and excitement. A well-written goal is worth gold.

Mortal Sin #5 is a lack of clear accountability specifying who will do what by when. Too many planners create strategic plans that stop at high-level strategy and don't include specific action steps that articulate who by name will do what action by what specific date. They like to claim that if you go that deep, it's not strategic planning, it's tactical or operational planning. I laugh at that ridiculous nonsense. Those are the same people whose plans die in three to six months. Sure, there are a myriad of books that support their viewpoint—but the authors of those planning processes are stuck in a time warp. Traditional, old school strategic planning—which is still today employed by most—does not include action plans. I love being a contrarian on this point—even being criticized for it doesn't bother me—because I know my clients will enjoy implementation success, not failure, because I insisted on taking the strategy down to the action level where the rubber meets the road. In the end they thank me for it and don't want to go back to their old way.

Wright

What about regular reviews of those action plans? Should that factor in?

Houcek

Wow, you're a mind-reader. That's actually **Mortal Sin #6**, which is having no frequent and regular check-ups to monitor ongoing progress. That old school model I referred to—that didn't include any action plans to begin with—usually calls for the planning group to reconvene in six months for a mid-year review. Sometimes it's scheduled after four months, but never more frequently than that. Turns out, that's suicide. A lesson I learned a long time ago when doing employee performance reviews only once a year, was that most employees took action on major initiatives in the eleventh and twelfth month because they knew the review was coming. They felt no pressure to begin before that.

My remedy: do reviews quarterly. But even then, action was often delayed until the third month of the quarter. Next remedy: do reviews once a month. Even with this frequency, action was sometimes delayed until the second half of the month, but it was still happening with greater urgency than once a year or once a quarter. The lesson it taught me was that "progress checks" on important initiatives should occur *early and often* and with religious zeal. Same concept applies to strategic planning. Inspect what you expect—*frequently.* Never less than monthly. And don't listen to the blowhards who claim that's micro-managing. It's not—it's responsible leadership.

Mortal Sin #7 is having no consequences or penalties for non-performance. In my experience, this is the terrain most leaders don't enjoy crossing. Leaders love to wear the white hat and talk about the upsides of success—the reward systems, recognition, bonuses, profit sharing, etc.—but truly hate talking about the downsides of failure. It's outside their comfort zones because it means having confrontational conversations with employees. Sure, it's much more fun to be well loved, admired, and popular, but one of the necessary attributes of effective leadership is dealing with non-performance head-on. People often fool themselves into believing they practice accountability, but they don't. If there are no consequences for non-performance, there is no accountability. Period. And because doling out consequences is uncomfortable for most, they avoid it. As a result, they have no accountability, which leads to weak execution, which ultimately causes the plan to die. It's predictable. The solution? Better wake up, step outside your comfort zone, and put in place some true consequences for non-performance. It's not as hard or uncomfortable as it sounds—and the results are incredible. Do it . . . get used to it . . . and before long, constructive confrontation will be *within* your comfort zone. Now, you're being an effective leader.

Mortal Sin #8 is failure to get look-me-in-the-eye commitment to a plan and its execution. I learned this the hard way. Have you ever summarized a group discussion by saying something like, "Okay, so are we all in agreement that our decision should be X [whatever your X is]?" Then you look around the table, pause a few seconds, and seeing no one in obvious disagreement, you say, "Good, then that's the way we'll go." Now, as you leave the meeting, you actually *think* you have group agreement, that everyone had their say, and action will happen accordingly. But of course, action does *not* happen accordingly.

This happened to me too many times until I woke up to the fact that it was my fault, not theirs. I was inadvertently and unintentionally giving them permission to be non-committal by not requiring a confirmation of support—either verbally or in writing—from each one. Committing that sin caused—as most others do—lousy implementation. But getting that look-me-in-the-eye commitment is so easy, and in a meeting with the importance of a strategic planning session—upon which a company's future success or failure rests—it is something I now require.

Wright

As I hear you define these planning mistakes, it all sounds so logical. But earlier, you said that about 80 percent of businesses don't have any kind of a written plan. Why do so many leaders allow planning to go unattended?

Houcek

For a variety of reasons, and your question is a great segue way to:

Mortal Sin #9: concocting flimsy excuses for *not* planning. I hear all kinds of unfounded reasons, like "The timing's not right" with no explanation for what they feel the right timing *would* be . . . or, "We're waiting for the customer research to be done" or, "Our financial projections for next year aren't yet complete." *That* one floors me. A strategic plan can be done *either before* or *after* the financial projections are done . . . but in my opinion, the best option is: *plan first, financial projections follow.* Why? Because doing it in reverse suggests a belief that available money should be the key driver of your strategy. In other words, if we can't afford it, we won't do it, no matter how good it is. That's backward—it'll put a ceiling on growth and you'll never realize your full potential.

The most wildly successful entrepreneurs know that if you have a killer idea, you *find* the money to afford it. If you're really passionate about it, you'll be amazed at your own creativity for identifying money sources. And very often, the money is right there in your existing business, without any need to borrow. You're probably putting money behind something that isn't paying off and probably won't, so why not kill it completely and re-direct all those resources to the new strategy? Some areas of a business must, at times, give their lives for other areas.

At any rate, none of these are good reasons for not planning. They're excuses. The fact is, there is really no bad time for planning. I had a personal experience as a corporate president in which we went through a horrible stretch of low cash, client unrest, and loss of a couple of key people, so I called off our monthly planning meetings for four consecutive months while we attacked these problems. My logic was, we've got our hands full, so don't make the leadership team spend time in those meetings.

As we eventually emerged from the crisis, I re-engaged the team meetings to get us back on track, and got summarily crucified by my direct reports for canceling the meetings. "We couldn't figure out why you cancelled those meetings," they said. "With all the crises exploding, we needed the meetings more than ever to talk things through, to deal with our plan, and stay focused."

When I told them I thought I was making the right decision to not take their minds off the immediate problems, they responded, "We would have met late on a weeknight, or come in on Sunday, or done whatever we had to do. We needed each other's voice, support, and commitment."

That experience taught me a valuable lesson: winners stay the course of dealing with the tough subjects, and by all means talk things through—no matter what hailstorm is occurring. To not talk, to not plan, to not follow-up with rigid regularity—especially in turbulent times—is suicide. My bad judgment had been a morale-killer, and the wisdom of their thinking was blinding. I apologized and thanked them for their candor. The lesson was well learned, and you can bet I never did that again.

Wright

Rick, thanks for sharing all nine planning flaws. They're enlightening, to say the least. I can see where they would hold a company back. So now let's jump ahead into the *solution*—the *right* way to tackle strategic planning—so that great ideas *can* get implemented. What are your suggestions?

Houcek

I have many. And so that I don't overlook the obvious, let me start by simply saying: if the nine sins I've discussed can truly deal a mortal blow to successful implementation, then the *opposite* of *each* of them must hold a secret to success.

So the process I'll outline will summarily turn negatives into positives. These are elements I use in my Power Planning™ strategic retreat process that, I'm proud to say, gets rave reviews from my clients, many of whom have used other facilitators or processes in the past. They tell me that mine stands alone in strategic and implementation effectiveness—music to my ears.

Here we go. First, the only time a one-person-created plan works is when a new business is being launched and there *is* only one person—the founder. But for an ongoing enterprise already up and running, it's much smarter to assemble a team to create the plan together. I suggest gathering a small team of ideally seven to ten individuals who represent every area and every person in the company. Leave no one unspoken for. If your management team only has four or five, then consider adding a few ad-hoc members who might only serve a one-year term, then be rotated off for new blood to come on to round out the team to a higher number. You need a certain level of energy in the room. Too few people won't cut it, and too many will overpower it. And yes, it's okay and encouraged to invite individuals at lower levels in the organization. I've had shop foremen on the team who made incredible contributions to the plan and who then became "ambassadors of management" to the shop floor workers. That's a huge *bonus* payoff.

Next, it's best to go off-site—even out of town—to get away from the daily distractions of fires burning, phones ringing, e-mail, faxes, and other meetings. You want a captive audience whose only focus is *the future*—and creating a plan to harness it. By far, the best locations are conference centers because they're built for one purpose—meetings. And you'll need every inch of wall space to hang flip chart sheets. Don't be tempted to go to your country club—they don't allow expensive paintings to be taped over. Even worse is a bed and breakfast, which is great for a romantic weekend, but lousy for a strategy meeting. And plan on two days with no one going home the middle night. Again, you want a captive audience

The reason for a *team*-created approach is that it's a big contributor to getting effective and long-lasting implementation of the plan. To me, implementation is the key to strategic planning success. This may shock you, but implementation is far more important than the strategy itself. Vince Lombardi once designed a new play, reviewed it with his offense, then threw it out when one of the eleven starters didn't understand. He knew that effective implementation was the key. Better to have mediocre plays with stellar, flawless execution than slick, razzle-dazzle plays with everyone not on board. Same is true here. Buy-in, buy-in, buy-in; I cannot stress it enough.

Wright

You mentioned earlier that CEOs who facilitate the meeting are asking for trouble. Who should do it if not the CEO?

Houcek

Very true, they'll be fooled into thinking the group has bought in, but will be surprised to learn—later of course, never at the meeting itself—that implementation is suffering and that few, if any, really bought into the plan in the first place.

The facilitator should be an outsider to the company—someone not emotionally vested in the outcome of the plan. An insider—even if not the CEO—will be influenced by which department he works in, who his friends are, who's mad at who, and is unlikely to be courageous enough to hit those issues head-on in the meeting. An outsider should be someone with exceptional people skills; but at the same time, someone with the guts to deal with these white elephant topics *during* the meeting. The facilitator, being an impartial third party, can concentrate on the process and can ask the tough questions others might fear to ask. Facilitating a dynamic planning session is a learned skill, by the way, that is developed over time. Trust it only to a trained professional. I must admit, I have a bias toward people who have spent considerable years inside the business world versus lifelong academics who teach business, but haven't lived it.

Let's talk about the retreat itself. Two full days off-site is really all that's needed and believe it or not, an exceptional plan can be *created completely* in that brief time. To be effective, the process used—and this is critical—must have a two-fold blend of both strategy development *and* specificity and commitment regarding execution. This is a key area in which most strategic planning "processes" I've seen, quite frankly, suck. Why? Because they deal way too much with strategy alone and too little, if any, with implementation. Do the facilitators of these processes really think the strategy is going to execute itself? Sadly, I'm left to infer they must, because they seem to ignore execution. Many processes take far longer than two days; the traditional planning model takes up to four months to complete and results in a 200- or 300-page binder that never gets read or referred to a second time. Worse, it has no action plan whatsoever—nothing that clearly articulates who by name will do what specifically by what date specifically. This is a mandate with me: every goal needs a clearly articulated action plan identifying major milestones with name responsibility and due dates for every single action step, bar none.

My Power Planning process, by contrast, ends up in a twenty-five-page or less plan, which clearly articulates a critical seven-point Strategic Direction bought into by the full retreat team—that becomes your Constitution—*and* specific goals, action steps, people responsible, and due dates to *ensure* the seven-point strategy is lived out—all complete by the end of day two. It's a perfect blend of *both* strategy *and* implementation—and I won't lead a planning session with any other process.

When you leave out the implementation piece, here's the downward spiral that happens next: the plan nose-dives in three to six months. It doesn't get talked about again, morale slowly deteriorates, you're at risk of losing your eagles, and your leadership abilities will be called into question. Not a good set of outcomes.

Wright

Wow, those *are* scary and not a place any CEO wants to end up. What about *after* the retreat? Tell us about a system for follow-up.

Houcek

This is critical for success.

The same team that met for the off-site retreat should meet once a month for a few hours to do three important things: check progress on actions steps that came due in the last thirty days, hold each other accountable for non-performance, and discuss any needed changes to the remainder of the plan going forward. In other words, don't use indelible ink on the plan. Good plans are fluid, not rigid and unbending. They allow you to adapt to changes in the marketplace. Your goals won't change very often, but your actions steps may. To meet less than once a month is asking for trouble. I used to do quarterly meetings, but realized that is too infrequent, and actions get put off until right before the meeting, which may mean more than two months might pass before action even begins. Monthly meetings mean more frequent attention to action steps.

Another key point is, don't hire a facilitator to write the plan for you. This is suicide of the highest order. Why would anyone internal—who had no authorship of the plan—have any real interest in implementing *that* plan? That's even worse than a CEO-created plan because at least the CEO works there—the facilitator doesn't. In short order, folks will lose interest in a plan created by an outsider. This begs the question: what is the facilitator's real job? Answer: not to author or create the plan, but to be a tour guide though a participative process in which the team creates its own plan. This requires the facilitator to check his or her ego at the door, and let go of the attachment to authoring the plan. The facilitator brings the *process;* the team creates the *content.*

Wright

You mentioned that the team must "hold each other accountable for non-performance." Go deeper on this, please.

Houcek

Accountability is where the rubber meets the road. My clients tell me that never before with any facilitator or process have they installed the accountability measures I insist on. This is the last element of the retreat process, and it gets discussed at the end of day two. In a nutshell, it must include clear consequences for non-performance or you don't even have accountability—you just *think* you do. I won't even accept a facilitation engagement if the CEO tells me, "We don't need that, we're pretty good about getting things done." He or she may believe that, but in my experience, *every* team needs firm accountability that includes consequences for non-performance. Leave this out and it's a recipe for implementation failure. And consequences, just like the plan itself, are best when created by the team, not jammed down their throat by the CEO or facilitator.

The facilitator should not insist on what the specific consequences should be, just that the team creates some with real teeth that they can live with. The final accountability piece is a written agreement signed by all at retreat's end that pledges each person's support of the plan and a willingness to bear the consequences they agreed on if they don't perform as promised. With all this in place, *now* you've got a plan with solid muscle behind it. The best news is that these plans get implemented.

Wright

Rick, it's clear to me that a skilled facilitator is essential to making all this happen. For company leaders who are on a "facilitator search," tell us what criteria and characteristics they should look for.

Houcek

I'm asked this all the time. And I can tell you that as a former corporate president myself, we used outside facilitators, so my selection criteria are based on my own real-life experience of what I know is important.

To start, a first-time facilitator is not a good idea. This retreat is your single-most important company meeting of the year, are you really willing to trust the outcome to a rookie? Someone who has been trained to lead meetings is clearly preferred. I'd also look for:

- Someone who has the guts to push and to ask tough, challenging outside-the-box questions
- Someone who has been in business and has a head for business versus a lifelong academic
- Someone with enough restraint to let the team create its own plan—not create his or her plan for them
- Someone who does one-on-one interviews with each retreat participant before the retreat—these are critical to retreat success—and surprisingly many facilitators don't consider these important
- Someone whose process requires the plan to be created during the retreat, not after
- Someone who has client references who will verify that their plans are getting implemented, and didn't die after three to six months. Remember, lousy implementation is the single-biggest reason for plan failure—so you want to know if this person has a history of helping to create realistic plans that can be implemented.
- Someone, I believe, who offers a written, money-back guarantee for pre-agreed deliverable or results. Call me

crazy, but I just have this simple bias that says, if you won't stand behind your work, won't offer a guarantee, and won't put it in writing—no matter what product or service you sell—you should not be allowed to do business in America. And I'm shocked at how few businesses actually do have written guarantees. Congress puts so many ridiculous restrictions on business that are unnecessary and make it difficult to succeed, but the *one* restriction they *should* put on every business is to have a written, iron-clad, money-back customer satisfaction guarantee of some sort—they don't.

Wright

I know *you* facilitate the Power Planning process, Rick, but being only one person, your availability must be limited. Are there others?

Houcek

Yes, I actually license other professional consultants, coaches, trainers, ex-CEOs, and former corporate executives to learn, use, and facilitate Power Planning. And I train them to deliver it with professionalism, clarity, and integrity. So I'm duplicating myself by creating a "flock of eagles" to help businesses everywhere to bring this dynamic planning tool into their companies. There just isn't enough of one person to go around—yet the market demand is tremendous. Anyone who's interested in becoming a Power Planning licensee should go to www.PowerPlanningFreeReport.com to get a Special Report that spells out the details. I'm always looking for another eagle to soar with. But beyond that, I still lead Power Planning retreats myself and I'm as passionate about it today as I was the day I started.

Wright

Well, Rick, this has been a most informative session. I doubt any company leader interested in strategic planning could read your comments and not walk away with tangible value. Any final parting thoughts?

Houcek

Yes, two: The Power Planning process, I've found, is best suited for small and mid-size companies—specifically entrepreneurs *and* autonomous divisions, subsidiaries, and regional offices of large corporations.

Second, I'm often asked: *Is there any industry for which Power Planning won't work?* Answer: no. Success isn't dictated by the category of business; it's determined by one thing only—the style of the leader. Power Planning will *not* work for leaders who are dictators or autocrats, who intend to fake team involvement only to later veto parts of the plan they don't like, who don't believe strategic planning can succeed, and who only need a business plan to get outside funding.

It will work *only* for leaders who have a participative, inclusive style with their top team, who believe strategic planning can succeed if done right and implemented well, who won't delete critical elements from the process, and who are willing to install firm, tough, line-in-the-sand accountability measures.

Wright

Rick, this has been an exceptional interview. Thank you so much for joining us in *Getting Things Done: Keys to a Successful Business,* and for offering so many powerful ideas to our readers.

Houcek

My pleasure, David, thank you.

About the Author

RICK HOUCEK'S singular company purpose is: *to provide high-octane, world-class strategic planning systems for business and life*, helping Top Gun leaders, teams, and individuals to succeed "on purpose, most of the time," rather than "by accident, some of the time." He does this in five primary ways: (1) facilitating his *Power Planning*™ strategic planning retreats for small and mid-size companies, (2) licensing the use of his Power Planning system to other consultants, coaches, and trainers, (3) leading his *Passion Planning*™ workshops for ambitious individuals on self-motivation, personal life planning and goal-setting, (4) delivering high-energy motivational keynotes, and (5) one-on-one success coaching.

He has coached entrepreneurs, CEOs, presidents, and senior executives for over ten years, and is former president of Ross Roy Advertising, an Atlanta ad agency and division of the $700 million Ross Roy Group. A University of Missouri graduate, he is a member of the National Speakers Association and has been recognized in *Who's Who Among U.S. Executives* and *Who's Who in Georgia.*

Rick is married and passionately devoted to his soul mate, Robbie, and he adores his awesome grown twins, Val and Chip. He has four fanatical life passions: his family, his personal health and fitness, helping others prosper through his business and friendships, and playing competitive baseball on a traveling men's team.

Rick Houcek, President
Soar With Eagles, Inc.
5398 Hallford Drive
Atlanta, Georgia 30338
Phone: 770.391.9122
Fax: 770.393.0076
E-mail: Rick@SoarWithEagles.com
www.SoarWithEagles.com
www.PowerPlanningFreeReport.com

Chapter 5

JOE CALLOWAY

THE INTERVIEW

David E. Wright (Wright)

Today we are talking with Joe Calloway. Joe is a restaurant owner, a business author, and a branding consultant whose client list reads like a Who's Who in business from newspapers in Sweden, Hotels in Great Britain, and computer companies in South Africa to the world brands like American Express and IBM. He's a guest lecturer with both the Graduate School of Business at the University of Tennessee and the Center for Professional Development at Belmont University. A recent issue of *Sales and Marketing Management Magazine* calls Joe "an expert on developing customer focused teams," and a National Customer Service Advisory Board called Joe "one of the most innovative and compelling people in the service industry." Joe's new book, *Becoming a Category of One*, has been released by John Wiley & Sons Publishing. He speaks frequently on business competition and he has been inducted into the Speakers Hall of Fame. Joe is nationally known as a straight talking expert on how to compete and win in today's market place.

Joe, welcome to *Speaking of Success*!

Joe Calloway (Calloway)

David, it's great to be with you.

Wright

Your book is called *Becoming a Category of One.* What does it mean to be a category of one? (That's a great title by the way.)

Calloway

Thank you. Let me tell you where I came up with it. I was working with a group in South Africa—you mentioned South Africa in your introduction. It was an international sales convention of a company, and I had the group working on an exercise, which is something that really anybody can do when they're trying to generate new ideas for their business.

Quite simply, what you do is think of a place where you are a customer. You absolutely love this business. This could be a restaurant, your dry cleaners, where you get your car fixed, it doesn't matter, just some place where you love to do business. Step two is, in ten words or less, what is it this business does that you find so powerful and so compelling? Step three is to think, "Well, okay, let me take what they do and apply it to my business even though we may be in totally different endeavors. What is it they are doing that we need to do more of?

Back to the story in South Africa. It is interesting because here we are in South Africa and there were people from forty different countries in the audience. The woman whose story really, really got my attention was from (of all places) west Texas. She said, "The business I'm thinking of is a little place called Walls Feed Store." I said, "Okay. What do they do at Walls Feed Store that's so powerful?" She said, "Well, my husband and I have a ranch with all kinds of animals— cats, cattle, dogs, horses, peacocks, llamas—it's like Noah's Ark. You name it, we've got it." She said, "As you might imagine in that part of Texas there are a lot of feed stores and you can buy feed from any of them. But Walls helps us take care of our animals. There's a difference." And it hit me. I thought, "You know, whatever this little feed store is doing, they have absolutely pulled off the ultimate in business because in the mind of that customer what they had done was taken themselves out of the very crowded category of feed stores and they had created a separate category and they were the only one in it." If you look back at what the woman said, it really gets to the heart of business. She said that there were a lot of feed stores but Walls "helps us take care of our animals." What that means is that store had been able to go from being seen as a commodity, meaning whatever you're selling, whatever service you're providing, I can get it anywhere, to creating a unique space in the mind of that customer that says, "Well, I can't get what these people do anywhere else." They do it in such a way that they separated themselves out. When I talk about *Becoming a Category of One*, that's where I got the idea.

Sometimes people will quite naturally think, "Well, that sounds good, but you know, I don't know if you can really literally pull that off." And my response to that is, "Well, okay, I'm going to name a product category and you tell me the category one." All I have to do, David, is say motorcycles and the automatic answer is Harley Davidson because Harley's done the same thing—they've created a mystique and something special around that machine that really goes beyond product.

A more recent example is I can say coffee shops and most people will say Starbucks. What Starbucks has done is a lesson for anybody in any kind of business. Starbucks has taken the simplest of commodities, the coffee bean—granted it's a great coffee bean, don't get me wrong, I'm not selling short the idea of product quality—and wrapped it with an experience that creates a category of one. You've got to have that. Starbucks starts with a really great product, but charging 2, 3, 4, or 500 percent more than most other coffee shops isn't just the product—it's that they have surrounded this product with an experience that consists of big cushy chairs, Internet connections, the people behind the counter who, if you are a regular, start fixing your coffee the second you walk in the door because they know what you want, and music that they play in the stores that you can actually buy and take home with you. So that's where the idea came from and that's what it's really all about.

Wright

If I were trying to become a *category of one* in whatever I was going to do, is the first step more introspective than anything else?

Calloway

Well, I'll tell you something. The first step, David, is even more introspective than that. It's funny. When I was researching the book, the basis of the book was looking for the *category of one* companies and looking for the threads they all have in common. In other words, what is it that these extraordinary companies do that any of us can do? One thing kept coming up, and it was not something I was looking for. It really gets to the heart of the word that you just used—introspective. All of these extraordinary companies were able to point to a specific kind, or in some cases a series, of specific moments in time when they quite simply, yet quite powerfully, made a concrete decision to take their business to another level. Every company talks about getting better and going to the next level, but very, very few companies actually make the decision and the commitment to do it. And there's a difference. It's not just semantics. There's a subtle but incredibly powerful difference. What I have found is that very few companies, and I don't care whether it's a 10,000- or 50,000-employee company, or a two-person company, very few businesses actually sit down and have an eye-to-eye, gut level conversation around the topics of: How good do we want to be? How far do we want to take this? How much fun do we want to have? How much success do we want to create? How much service do we want to give? There's just this unspoken assumption that, "Well, of course, we want to be a great company." But that's a dangerous assumption. It really takes getting it on the table and having a confronting conversation about who wants to go. The first chapter of the book ended up being titled, *We Just Decided to Go* because I came to the realization that the mandatory first step is making this decision to go, yet oddly enough, it's the step not taken in some of those companies.

Wright

So how important is innovation in sustaining success today?

Calloway

Well, innovation is almost a requirement. It's inherent in the process of improving your business because there's an old saying, "Insanity is doing the same thing you've always done and yet expecting a different result." Well, if you're going to take your business to the next level, whatever that means to you, then almost by definition that means you're going to have to change. Even though I think virtually everybody out there agrees intellectually, with the idea that you have to constantly change in order to stay competitive, on a gut level most people are still resistant to change. There's a statement that I use with people to provoke some thought around change, and it's this: Past success can be, and usually is, the enemy of future success. It's a really difficult and confrontive idea to deal with. It's confrontive for me. The idea is that whatever got you to the level of success where you are now, whatever has worked to get you to this point may in fact be the very thing that's keeping you from getting to the next level.

A lot of people say that Peter Drucker is the greatest business thinker of our time. He said something that really made me think. He said, "Success always makes obsolete the very behavior that created it." He also said that whenever you see a successful business that is successful over a long period of time, you have people within that business who are making courageous decisions. I think courage often comes down to innovation. Innovation by definition means you go first.

I'll often talk with people who say, "Well, we're very innovative in our company because we benchmark our competition, and we look at what the best companies in our field are doing, and then we do that, too." Well, gang, that's not innovation. That's copying. If you do that it assures that you're never going to be better than second place. I'm not saying that there's anything wrong with knowing what your competition's doing, you want to know that too.

Innovation means you have to do those things that make people look at you and say, "Well, wait a minute; you can't do that in this business. We've never done that! This is not the sort of thing that people in our business do." But those are the only ideas that are significant enough to ultimately have an impact competitively. It's to do those things that have never been done before. Quite literally, that is the definition of innovation.

Wright

There's a lot of talk, Joe, about brand these days. Obviously I know what branding is, but what does "brand" really mean?

Calloway

Well, it's interesting. I think the traditional definition of "brand" is one that includes things like your logo, the name of your company, the slogan that you use, and your advertising. That's what is traditionally thought of as branding. It's taking an idea and slapping it on top of your company. My approach to brand is that you build your brand from the inside out.

The definition of brand that I came up with that I think is incredibly useful for any business of any size is this: your brand is your customers' perception of what it's like to do business with you. Another way of putting it is to say that your brand is your customers' experience of doing business with you. In other words, if I'm talking to one of your customers and she happens to mention that you know she did some business with you and I say, "Well, what's it like to do business with them?" Whatever she says next, that's your brand. If I want to know what your brand is, I won't even ask you—I'll ask your customers. And so that's why my belief is that everything, and I mean that literally, David, every single decision you make in your business should be looked at with the question of, "How does this decision affect the experience of my customers when they do business with me?" Everything is about customer experience. It's not just about the product you sell. It's not just about the service that you provide. It's about everything that surrounds that product. That goes right back to what I was saying about Starbucks. The Starbucks brand is about much more than coffee. The Harley Davidson brand is about much more than a motorcycle. It's about what it is like to do business with you that ultimately becomes the differentiator between you and your competition.

Wright

Right. As you were talking about that it reminded me of something. I frequent a restaurant in my town where the food is not particularly all that good and certainly not as good as some others. I wondered, this has just been a few months ago, why do I keep going there? So after a little bit of introspection, I came up with the fact that I probably go there for the same reason that Norm went into Cheers—everybody knows my name.

Calloway

That's an interesting point that you bring up. James Beard, who was recognized as one of the great—possibly the greatest—chef of the twentieth century, was interviewed once by a food magazine. He was asked, "Mr. Beard, what's your favorite restaurant?" His answer was, (and you can apply this to any business of any kind anywhere), "My favorite restaurant is the one where they know me." Knowing your customer and creating an experience that becomes a relationship is as powerful a differentiator as there is in business today. It's huge.

Wright

What do you think is the biggest competitive issue that most businesses face today?

Calloway

It's exactly what we're talking about—it's the challenge of differentiating. Differentiating means demonstrating a difference between you and your competition. Differentiation is the answer to the question. I see a hundred different businesses that do what you do. They all do it well. They all do it for about the same price. So given that, why should I do business with you? David, that is the toughest question in business to answer. You ask just about any business what the difference is between them and their competition, and one thing you will often hear is, "It's our people." Well, okay that's probably true. But my follow-up question is, "What does that mean? When you say it's your people, what is it that your people are literally willing or able to do that your competition is literally not willing or able to do?"

When you take it to that level, that's where a lot of businesses start hemming and hawing and stammering a little bit because they're a little hard pressed to come up with an answer. They say, "Well, we've got great people." I'm sure you do, but your competition says *they've* got great people. Tell me, specifically, what is it that you do that your competition doesn't do? If you say, "Well, we give great service," then does it mean that if your competition can solve a given problem in three hours, you can solve it in thirty minutes? It gets down to being able to quantify and go beyond a slogan in telling me why I should do business with you. I'll tell you what, though, the key is usually going to be in the people. It's very, very difficult to differentiate with a product any more. The nature of technology today is such that if you come out with a product that truly is different or better than your competitors', it's going to take them probably all of five minutes to catch up with you. So you have to find a way to differentiate somewhere in the relationship.

Wright

Going back to the example I gave about the restaurant where everybody knows my name. In my opinion, they actually have 100, if not more, customers inside the restaurant who are really working for them and not getting paid. Not only do they speak to me as I go in the door, but before I get to the back room where I generally sit, I have spoken to three or four lawyers or six or seven secretaries. It's like they are all waiting there for me and I'll disappoint them if I don't show up. It's infectious what these people are doing who work for this restaurant.

Calloway

What they've done is they've created a space in which business has become an act of friendship. I defy you to name any kind of business anywhere, and I'm even including in that high level business-to-business transactions, where making it an act of friendship is not appropriate. I want to give credit where credit is due. A friend of mine named Jim Cathcart (as far as I know) came up with the idea that business, when done correctly, is an act of friendship. I think this speaks volumes to the nature of what today's customer is looking for, regardless of the kind of business that they're involved with.

Wright

It seems like every company claims to exceed their customers' expectations. In your opinion, how many of them really do that?

Calloway

Virtually none; here's why. It's funny, David. We go through phases of slogans that become popular. I think the single most popular advertising slogan out there today is, "We exceed our customers' expectations." Businesses say this without really giving it much thought at all. My first question to anybody who says that is, "Well, do you have any clue how high your customers' expectations are?" The expectations of today's customer are infinitely higher than they've ever been in history.

I was doing business with a credit card company that I'm a big fan of. Not too long ago I called them up to track down the details about a particular charge that I had made. The young woman who pulled up my account was very friendly and very professional. She gave me the information I needed and she gave it to me quickly. At the end of the conversation they had built in a little customer survey. She said, "Mr. Calloway, do you mind if I ask you a question?" I said, "Of course not." She said, "Did I exceed your expectations today?" I said, "No, you didn't." And I could almost hear her jaw dropping on the other end of the phone line. She immediately said, "Oh my gosh, what did I do wrong?" I said, "You didn't do anything wrong. You were terrific. You met my expectations. You did exactly what I pay you for." What's funny to me is that there are businesses that will provide a good product and good service, and then they sit back and expect people to just fall over with delight because you did what they paid you to do.

If you give me a good product and good service and you're friendly and all that, that's fine. That's pretty much what I'm paying for. In all fairness, I'll tell you something about that same credit card company in a totally different situation. I had lost my credit cards. I called the two credit card companies that were involved. They both said, "We'll get you your replacement cards immediately." The first company sent me my replacement cards; it took about ten days for them to arrive, which was fine. The other company, I made the call to within thirty minutes of the first one, had cards delivered to me by UPS at my office the next morning. Now that exceeded my expectations.

I was not expecting that. I'll tell you the other thing that it did. It was a clear differentiator between them and their competitor. They paid for UPS to have those cards delivered to me the next morning. That made a big impression. So number one, it was a differentiator and number two, it did exceed my expectations. But if you're going to exceed my expectations, you've got to go way beyond doing a good job because that's what I'm paying you to do.

Wright

What do think are some ways that companies can achieve consistency of performance? I know there are a lot of people who will be reading this book who will want to know what they can do. Can you help us out there?

Calloway

Yes, the how to's, David, come down to basically three or four things. I think the frustration of a lot of people is that they hear the stories and they say, "You know, that's all well and good, but how do you do it?" There's good news and there's bad news. The bad news is there is no template. There are no ten steps that I, or anybody else, can hand a business and say, "Look, here's ten steps. Do these things; it's easy." It's not easy. It's simple though. The way to achieve category one status, the way to becoming extraordinary is simple, but it's not easy. Quite frankly, every extraordinary company of any size that I've seen, that I've done business with, that I've written about, that I've researched, all have this in common. They figured it out on their own.

Now, having said that, there are some basic truths. There are some things that run through all of these companies. I'll give you two or three of them. One is about knowing who we are. By knowing who we are, I don't mean what we sell. I mean who we are as people and how we want to do business with other folks, the way we want to treat each other, and the way we want to treat our customers. The really successful companies, when they hire a new employee, way before they start talking the job description, they spend a lot of time talking about what kind of people they are at that company. They talk about values. They talk about what's important. It really comes down to culture. The companies that had decided they are going to be a pleasure to work with, or that say, "We're going to be the best part of each customer's day," that's the sort of thing that they talk about all the time.

That brings me to the second point. Beyond who we are is I think about leadership. I'm not talking about management here. I'm talking about leadership, which I think is a different thing. Managing involves making the organization function properly. Leadership is this idea of constantly reminding everyone of who we are, remember what's important, remember how we treat people, remember who we are.

A third element that flows from that is consistency. There are some companies that, if they were truthful in their advertising, they'd say, "Feel lucky? Well, come on in 'cause it depends on who you get." That's a brand killer. If it depends on who I get in your store, in your restaurant, in your consulting business, whatever it may be, then you've got a big problem. The really extraordinary companies that are consistent (e.g., it doesn't matter who you get on the phone, it doesn't matter what sales clerk or cash register you go to, it doesn't matter who you run into in the aisles of the store) are going to have a consistency of performance that runs through the entire organization.

I guess the fourth element would involve everything we were saying about differentiation. That ultimately comes down to how we treat people.

There was a service technician in our home a few months ago doing an inspection just to be sure everything's okay. The service technician knew that our little two-year-old daughter was upstairs taking a nap. He'd done the work outside. As he was coming back in the house, I saw him closing the sliding glass door. He did it in slow motion to be sure that he didn't make any noise. He turned around and saw me and whispered that he had finished the inspection. He said that everything was fine, and he'd let himself out the front door. When he went out the front door, he did the same thing—he closed the door in slow motion to keep from waking up the baby. You may say to yourself, "Well, that's not that big a deal." No, it's everything because he understood that his business was not about just inspecting the air conditioning unit. His business was about taking care of our home, and that involved everything down to whispering when you know the baby's taking a nap.

We try to make rocket science out of this stuff, and it basically comes down to the way you treat people. That's the essence of business.

Wright

What a great conversation, Joe. I always learn when I talk with you.

Calloway

It was a pleasure, David. I enjoy it every time.

Wright

I'm going to shamefully market this book, *Becoming a Category of One.*

Calloway

It's doing extremely well. We're just thrilled with the reception it's had and the reviews it's received. It's available in book stores, Amazon.com and barnes&noble.com.

Wright

Great! I am heading to our local bookstore to pick it up.

Today we've been talking with Joe Calloway, who is a business author and a branding consultant. He speaks all over the world—Great Britain, South Africa—and he talks a lot about branding, a lot about business, and a lot about leadership. He is also a guest lecturer at the University of Tennessee—my alma mater—and the Center for Professional Development at Belmont University.

Joe, thank you so much for being with us today. I really do appreciate the time you've taken with us.

Calloway

It was an absolute pleasure. Thank you.

About The Author

JOE CALLOWAY is a restaurant owner, a business author, and a branding consultant whose client list reads like a Who's Who in business from newspapers in Sweden, Hotels in Great Britain, and computer companies in South Africa, to the world brands like American Express and IBM. He's a guest lecturer with both the Graduate School of Business at the University of Tennessee and the Center for Professional Development at Belmont University. A recent issue of *Sales and Marketing Management Magazine* calls Joe "an expert on developing customer focused teams," and a National Customer Service Advisory Board called Joe "one of the most innovative and compelling people in the service industry." Joe's book, *Becoming a Category of One*, was released by John Wiley & Sons Publishing. He speaks frequently on the business competition and he has been inducted into the Speakers Hall of Fame. Joe is nationally known as a straight talking expert on how to compete and win in today's market place.

Joe Calloway
P.O. Box 158309
Nashville, Tennessee 37215
Phone: 615.383.2249
Fax: 615.383.4964
www.joecalloway.com

Chapter 6

BARRY BANTHER

THE INTERVIEW

David Wright (Wright)
Today we're talking with Barry Banther who is a sought-after business advisor and an inspirational speaker. He helps leaders earn the right to be followed by how they communicate *openness, empathy, and encouragement* to their associates and their customers. Barry draws from thirty years of experience as a former corporate COO, college president, and public leader. He served an unprecedented four terms as chairman of the Florida State Board of Independent Colleges and Universities. This body of work, along with clients from among the Fortune 100, has earned him the highest designation as both a Certified Management Consultant (CMC) and Certified Speaking Professional (CSP). He is CEO of Banther Consulting and an avid trout fisherman in the mountains of western North Carolina.

Barry, what's the biggest barrier you have seen your clients face in getting things done?

Barry Banther (Banther)

Very few people have a problem getting things done. In fact, most people I have encountered are getting too much done! The problem is not "getting it done," the challenge is getting the "right things done."

Americans are working more hours per week today than ever before in our history. Few, if any, industrialized nations in the world put in as many hours as we do. But when we equate activity with progress we can get ourselves in trouble.

I was standing fifth in line recently at a rental car check-in. With so many people checking their bags it took forever to get my luggage. We had to wait for the rental car bus to fill up before we could leave baggage claim and now I'm standing in another line. What does it matter if your flight is on time if you can't get out of the airport for another hour?

But here is the real issue: there was one rental agent working at the counter and three standing nearby talking with each other! As I eavesdropped it became apparent they were trying to resolve a problem with the next week's schedule. They weren't wasting time on personal issues, this was a company problem, but they were solving the wrong problem. They were getting something done but it was not the right thing at the moment. Get the customers out the door and then solve next week's schedule!

The biggest barrier my clients face is clearly choosing what needs to get done now. But this first requires that somebody decide how the work is prioritized—how to choose among the "more than we can handle" things that need to get done.

Wright

Barry, what advice do you give people so they can make the best choice?

Banther

In addition to working more hours than any time in our history we are also bombarded with communication at an unprecedented rate.

In 1976 I was Executive Vice President of a nationwide corporation. I was responsible for broadcast stations from Baltimore to Los Angeles to Tampa. I had no personal computer, no cell phone, and no fax machine. If people wanted to communicate with me they had three choices: call me on the phone, write me a letter, or come to see me. Oh, for the simple life!

Today you can be e-mailed, called on the phone, messaged on your blackberry, called on your cell-phone, Web conferenced, stuck in a meeting, and you can still receive a fax or a page. And all within three minutes!

One thing hasn't changed—there are only twenty-four hours in a day, no more and no less. The phrase 24/7 has come to identify our dilemma. If time is constant then what separates the highly productive and profitable groups from the also-rans? The answer is as old as the scriptures: *Before you build a tower, sit down and count the cost.* There are seven questions I help my clients answer that will enable them to count the cost and get the right things done every time:

1. *What is our preferred method of communication with our clients/customers?*—Whether it's cell phone, land-line, or e-mail, how do we prefer our customers communicate with us? Whatever the answer, it is imperative that you clearly let customers/clients know the best way. A popular television psychologist, Dr. Phil, likes to say, "We teach people how to treat us." Leave it up to your customers/clients and they will try every means possible to get to you and it will create chaos in your company.

    Teach your customers/clients how to communicate with you and why that method will be in their best interest. Then in turn train your associates that when clients communicate using that media, respond instantly. It's okay to select a back-up method of communication and inform customers if they need to use that. But they should only use it because it's all that is available to them, not because we didn't respond to them when they used the preferred method.

    The preferred method used by customers/clients to contact you will probably vary within your company. Customer service may choose a phone call while accounting prefers an e-mail. Make a decision about this and train all customers and associates. Reward everyone who makes the right choice!

2. *What is our preferred method of communication within our company, between associates?*—I was sitting in an executive's office when his BlackBerry signaled a message. It was from someone in the next room. Granted, the person didn't want to disturb our meeting by walking in so he chose to send a message hundreds of miles in low orbit so

that he could get it to a receiver less than twenty feet away—but our meeting was still disturbed when the executive said, "Do you mind if I check this?"

If your company doesn't have a protocol for internal communication then you've got an age seven and under soccer team with dozens of bodies running toward the ball and trying to reach it!

Now, don't misunderstand me. There is no one best way to communicate internally but there can only be *one* preferred way that keeps one from wasting time fielding off dozens of electronic impulses simultaneously.

One client made this determination: If you are in the same building and you need an answer within the next three hours you must call on the company phone or walk to the person's office. If you need the decision by tomorrow then you can e-mail (or BlackBerry) it to be reviewed later. If you are not in the same building, then try the company phone first and use e-mail as the back-up. Cell phones are for emergency only

Your choices may be entirely different but you must create an agreed upon priority or you will have people constantly complaining that someone never got back to them, the message didn't go through, they didn't know it was needed now, etc. Or worse, you will waste time checking your phone messages, e-mail, and/or BlackBerry, and cell phone constantly so you don't "miss" something important.

3. *How do we determine what work has to get done today when there is so much that must be done today?*—The president of the company proudly walked me around introducing me to his staff crowded into cubicles in every corner. He lamented about his lack of "qualified applicants" and his need to add at least five more associates. My assignment was to help him figure out a way to improve the bottom line when the business was growing so fast.

It didn't take long for me to realize what was happening. Everyone was busy doing everything all day. They actually bragged to me that regardless of what their job description said, everybody just does what is necessary to satisfy customers. Noble thought but terribly misguided.

As the business grew his only option was to throw more people at his problems, like noticing that your car is about out of gas so you drive as fast as you can past gas stations hoping you can make it to your destination!

So, what's the solution? You have to get rid of that old job description and replace it with a living, dynamic instrument. Dale Carnegie Training refers to this as a "Position Results Description" and others call it a "Position Qualification Checklist." Whatever you call it, it contains a clear list of the results that must be achieved by whoever does that job. This instrument doesn't describe what you do but, rather, the results you must achieve. Once that is determined, then you can decide what you have to do each day to get those results. If you are choosing to do something that doesn't lead to those results then stop doing it! Maybe someone else should be doing that task but if it doesn't apply to what you have to achieve, you can't afford to be doing it.

One footnote: the leadership in your company has to be constantly reviewing and adjusting the results your individual team members are accountable for. When people know the results needed rather than just job tasks, they will be more apt to do the right thing and not just "some thing."

4. *How will you measure your success?*—Sounds like a silly question doesn't it? Just look at the bottom line, Barry! But a lot of people with strong bottom lines have found themselves quickly upside down. That's because the bottom line is a result not a measure.

If you want to get things done, then you have to decide how you will measure the things that are getting done and how they relate to your success measures. Ask every department leader to identify what he or she measures every day. Once those leaders have done that, challenge them to defend how every action by their associates contributes to those measures.

Some people will undoubtedly say that you can't measure what they do. Try this exercise: ask them to pretend that their jobs are being eliminated but you will give them five minutes to prove that the tasks they do all day have a direct bearing on their department's success. You will be amazed how quickly they come up with metrics for what they do. It's then your job to determine if those are the right metrics.

It's also about this time when you will get some push back from one of your leaders who complains that he or she is spending so much time measuring, evaluating, and adjusting the work that his or her work can't get done. Don't say anything, just look at the person in silence. Most leaders will get the message—measuring, evaluating, and adjusting is *their* job!

By the way, my client didn't even get beyond this fourth question before he realized he had too many associates, not too few. Once people understood the desired results and how to measure their work, they voluntarily stopped doing all those things that were burning up time and not nearly as important as they once thought.

5. *How do you continuously train your associates to get things done?*—I am not asking about industry conferences or university continuing education programs. I am inquiring about what your leaders do every day to train and re-train their teams to do the right thing and not just some thing.

Today the world of work is dynamic and the pressure for change comes from every angle. On-the-job training must be part of your daily routine. If you're not a golfer then forgive me, but the best example of this comes from the world of the Professional Golfers Association (PGA). Several years ago one of golf's best, Phil Mickelson, sought out some legendary teachers to help him improve his game. One of those was Dave Pelz. Pelz brought the mind of an analyst/scientist to his business of teaching. He responded to Mickelson that he would be willing to help him but it would mean practicing on the courses where the major tournaments are played a lot more often than he was used to.

Mickelson balked. He replied that he had played the Augusta National—site of the Masters—every spring, many times and knew the course well and saw no need to do more. Pelz had one question, "How's that working for you?" Mickelson relented and the rest is history. He has since one two Masters tournaments.

Someone in your organization has to be examining what everyone is doing every day and carving out moments to ask, "How can we do this better?" Whether it is a call center manager breaking down calls all day or the director of accounting watching how data gets posted. You have to become fanatical about finding opportunities to improve and providing an immediate opportunity for an associate to get better at that. This can often happen in just a matter of minutes.

Ask yourself these questions: Do you have associates doing tasks just as they did a year ago? Have your vendor requirements changed in the past year? Do your customers have different expectations than a year ago? How do you know that is still the most profitable way for that task to be done? If you can't answer these questions every week then chances are good you have associates doing something, but not necessarily the right thing or the best thing.

You can rest assured of this: There is someone or some group out there that wants to take your business away from you. They have access to more capital and, don't be offended, but they probably have access to smarter people than you do. They want to bring you down. Are you going to let them?

6. *What are you, as a leader, doing every week to listen to your customers?*—Talk about a question from the last century! But you would be surprised how many clients I have who believe that's important but who don't quite get around to doing it. If you are the president, the general manager, or the owner of your own enterprise, then the best thing you can do to get things done is to make listening to customers your number one priority.

Schedule some time every week to simply listen. No agenda. No new product or service to introduce. No matter to resolve.

I have a client in Atlanta whose president, Sid Mealor, has become a clear example of this. Sid began calling on clients every week. Long before we met he was close to his clients but now he was more purposeful about it. Recently, he told me about visiting a customer and hearing from him that if his company could get more favorable terms they might double their business with Sid's company. While the customer took a call, Sid excused himself and stepped outside. He quickly called his comptroller and credit manager to see if more favorable terms made sense. With a green light from them he returned to his customer and said, "Let's give it a try!" That is an example of a leader getting the right thing done—now!

He might have found out about this opportunity through his outside salesman who called on this customer, but the point is that Sid himself could take action to get it done. There was plenty he could have been doing back in his office but perhaps nothing that could have been more profitable.

You can't figure out which customer to listen to who might present an opportunity. You have to listen to them all (or at least the top several) routinely. Do this and you will be in the right place at the right moment to get something done that will make a difference.

7. *How do you reward associates for getting the right thing done?*—Every company has developed a rewards and recognition program. But the next generation of those programs must focus on rewarding associates for making the right choices. Your associates are faced with multiple choices every day. And it's not a matter of right or wrong but, rather, what's the best decision?

The McNichols Company, with branches all across America, is known as the "Hole Company" because they sell steel products (perforated, grip strut, wire cloth) with holes in them. Their brand is well known in their industry.

Throughout the year they announce "Hole Choice Awards." This tangible recognition goes to associates (they call them Hole Team Members) who, when faced with a choice, made the best one and got the right thing done. Scott McNichols, Executive Vice President and General Manager, likes to present the awards at a luncheon and with the suspense of the popular People's Choice Awards on television.

If you have answered the first six questions, then you probably have a good idea of the kinds of actions you want to recognize among your associates. For this to work you have to be consistent and make sure you are recognizing as many people as possible who are choosing between just doing something and doing the right thing.

As your leaders refine what needs to get done every day, make sure you adjust your recognition so that you are rewarding today what you want to see more of tomorrow.

Wright

Barry, it sounds like getting things done really depends on a proactive leader.

Banther

It begins and ends with leadership. If, as leader, you don't have a reputation for getting the right thing done and done now, then that's your biggest problem. But you can do something about it.

Bob Cardwell is President of the Castle Supply Company on the west coast of Florida. Recently, this company was recognized as Wholesaler of the Year. One key is Cardwell's commitment to get done today what needs to be done today. He arrives at work before anyone else on his leadership team and works through the big issues he thinks the company will face that day and the rest of the week. By the time everyone else is there he is ready to make decisions and empower associates to get the right thing done.

You may not be able to come in that early but you must find a way to do your prep work in time to be an example of a leader who can make decisions now. A dynamic workplace cannot wait while you sit behind closed doors and think about it.

Simply put, the leaders at every level have to be a role model of getting the right thing done—now.

Before they were leaders, most people were doers. Their companies recognized their ability to get things done in a timely and profitable manner. Consequently, they climbed the ladder of responsibility until they became a manager, vice-president, or perhaps even president. But they have to be careful. The skills that got them to where they are may not be the skills that can take them and their company to the next level.

Bill Couchenour was a successful Project Consultant and District Manager in Cogun Industries, one of America's premier builders of churches and houses of worship. Bill's ability to relate to his clients (they call them VSPs) won him numerous awards for surpassing sales goals. As a result, he became president of the company when his father retired.

With Project Consultants (salespeople) and District Managers all over the Midwest and eastern United States, Bill had to decide how to lead them in a tough economic market. The first temptation was to tell everybody how he did it and require them to do the same. It didn't take much time or reflection for that to be proven a bad idea.

Bill formed a leadership team of his District Managers. And he began to engage them in discussions about what it takes to help "ordinary men and women to accomplish extraordinary things." He took that mantra from one of his favorite authors, Peter Drucker.

In other words, Bill had to focus on getting different things done than he had in the previous decade as a frontline warrior. He now had to lead from the helm and that meant that to get things done, he had to inspire, encourage, and empower others who were still on the front line.

In the short run, Cogun might have had more immediate success if Bill had just written the handbook for performance and demanded the allegiance of everyone. But would that inspire anyone? Would that encourage anyone to attempt the difficult project that could become very profitable? No.

I realize it's much easier for me to speak about this than it was for Bill Couchenour to do it. Not everyone bought in. Some people just wanted to be told what to do. And others wanted to follow their own agenda. But successful leaders who leave a lasting legacy realize that their work is not about buildings or projects or new markets. Their work is about people and what they have to do to help them become leaders.

Try this exercise: Examine the work you have on your desk today. How much of that is product or task specific and how much is about listening to one of your younger managers? How much is about making sure some small task gets done and how much is about investing time with one of your leaders to make certain they believe in themselves and their ability?

I know from experience that it's easier just to do something that you can check off a list at the end of the day. Resist that temptation! Delegate everything you possibly can to someone else and focus your time on the people you lead. What will make them smarter? What will make them better? What will motivate them to find a new way to excite customers?

I mentioned earlier about those broadcast stations I was responsible for decades ago (Baltimore, Cincinnati, Toledo, Los Angeles, and Tampa). I had no cell phone or computer. A young man in his twenties recently asked me in amazement how I was able to monitor accounts receivable, payables, daily tasks, and the like without instant access. My answer to him was pretty simple, I had to trust people.

Because you and I have so many tools to monitor people with, we don't take the time to build trust. When I know that you trust me to make the best choice and get the right thing done, then that is liberating. And do you know what liberation does for the soul?

Some of you are thinking, if I liberate my team they will make a poor decision and I will be held accountable. You might be right. But cautious, looking over their shoulder to see what you think behavior will never result in stellar success. And neither you nor your team will win the big game.

There is risk for leaders to do what I am suggesting. But the greater risk is in doing what you have always done hoping that fate will smile on you. I have been dumped on by fate before . . . but it wasn't a smile! The old phrase from yesterday is still true—*we make our own weather!*

Examine yourself. What are you getting done today? What difference will it make a year from now? What could you do instead that might harness the untapped energy and enthusiasm of someone else? How you answer these questions will impact your legacy as a leader more than anything else you will do in the next twenty-four hours.

Wright

Barry, thank you for your insight on getting things done. One final question: what keeps you focused every day?

Banther

Every day is filled with two realities: opportunities and obstacles. I have learned through my own failures that the key is to see them both as the same thing—solving problems. And solving problems is the profession that I have chosen. Every solution to a problem reveals a new and often profitable opportunity. You can't have one without the other.

Over the past decade, what I get done every day has become much more focused. And it starts first thing in the morning. Since I was a young man I have tried to take time every morning to reflect on the day and thank the Lord for His blessings in my life and to seek guidance for the day. But in recent years that has changed a bit.

I still take that time every morning, even if it has to be done in an airport or riding down the highway with my eyes wide open! But I have been encouraged by a story from the Old Testament. Nehemiah was a civil servant in the court of an ancient king. He had heard that the walls of Jerusalem had been broken down and his brothers were attempting to rebuild them. He instantly wanted to go and help. But how could he? How could he ask the king for a leave of absence to do such a thing? He prayed early in the morning about his dilemma, just as many of us pray every morning and ask for help. But he took it one step further.

When Nehemiah was in front of the King and the King asked why he looked so troubled this was his chance to make his request. But before Nehemiah blurted out his problem the Scriptures record that he quickly prayed (with his eyes wide open and standing in front of his earthly king) and then made his request to the ruler.

You will have to read Nehemiah's story in the book that bears his name to find out what happened. But I learned from him to be in continuous reflection and I shoot a lot of quick prayers up as I am working with my clients. They don't realize it but I think they benefit from it.

I read where the late Dr. Norman Vincent Peale used to say under his breath repeatedly just before he was introduced to speak to an audience, "God love these people through me. Love these people through me." When I do this it rarely changes what I am getting done but it gives me renewed enthusiasm for the task at hand.

When I keep this attitude about myself it also helps me focus on even the small things that can have lasting importance in my life and the lives of my clients. And every now and then it gives me permission to set aside what I thought was critical and do something irrelevant like fishing with a friend!

In fact, that's one of the right things that I need to get done today, so if you will excuse me . . .

Wright

[Laughing] Thank you, Barry.

About the Author

BARRY BANTHER is a sought-after advisor and an inspirational speaker. He helps leaders earn the right to be followed by how they communicate *openness, empathy, and encouragement* to their associates and their customers. Barry draws from thirty years of experience as a former corporate COO, college president, and public leader. He served an unprecedented four terms as chairman of the Florida State Board of Independent Colleges and Universities. This body of work, along with clients from among the Fortune 100, has earned him the highest designation as both a Certified Management Consultant (CMC) and Certified Speaking Professional (CSP). He is CEO of Banther Consulting and an avid trout fisherman in the mountains of western North Carolina.

Barry Banther
Banther Consulting
1708 Gulf Beach Blvd.
Tarpon Springs, Florida 34689
Phone: 800.977.7234
E-mail: Barry@BarryBanther.com
www.BarryBanther.com

Chapter 7

Tom Bay, PhD

David Wright (Wright)

Today, our interview is with Dr. Tom Bay, PhD. He has thirty-five years of speaking experience nationally as well as internationally. He holds a master's degree and doctorate in both Media and Communications.

His main focus in his corporate training seminars and workshops is getting things done and being productive with the time you have available. He has inspired thousands of individuals to direct their energies inward for more productive, positive, and successful lives, keeping a balance in all parts of one's life both in the career and personal aspects. Life and work balance is the core of true success. He knows this concept since he has served his community and those about him by walking his talk. He has been elected to fifty-five boards of directors and asked to serve as chairman for fifty of those boards. All this has been accomplished while writing or contributing to seven books. Three of his books are sold internationally: *Rainbows, Whispers, and Shouts: Gifts in Thoughts; Change Your Attitude: Creating*

Success One Thought At A Time; and *Look Within or Do Without: 13 Qualities Winners All Share.*

We are proud to have Tom as one of our chapter authors in our recent publications: *Leadership: Helping Others to Succeed,* and *Mission Possible.*

It's my pleasure to welcome you, Tom, to *Getting Things Done: Keys to a Successful Business.*

Bay

Once again I am honored to be interviewed by you David. I have great respect for you and Insight Publishing. By the way, I'd like to add that "getting things done" is one of the keys to a successful life.

Wright

Tom, you seem to have such a passion for all your work based on time management. Please give us the basis for this passion and why time management?

Bay

Thanks, David for a great opening question.

No matter what we do with our lives, both personal and career, we all are equalized by the time we have available. We all have one and only one standard. This standard is worldwide and is easily overlooked. This standard is that we have only 1,440 minutes in a single day, no more and no less. Statements made such as, "When I have more time," "As soon as I have more time," "If only I had more time," etc. are not valid and never will be valid—no one can add more minutes to a day.

What's even more important is that the only day we have to work with is today. Yesterday is gone and tomorrow may never come. If you wake up today, this is the *only* day (1,440 minutes) you have to accomplish your tasks. Most don't recognize the true value of today. Often times we tend to fret over yesterday and what we didn't get done.

In a nutshell, here's my attitude: Let go of the past, you can't fix it or change it. Don't worry about the future. It's important to make plans but stop worrying and make the most of this one day—make it your best.

Here's another way to clarify what I call our three-day lives: Yesterday is a cancelled check. Tomorrow is a promissory note. Today is cash in hand. How you invest your cash in hand is how you get your return on investment.

Wright

It seems so simple but is it realistic?

Bay

Excellent question, David. It is realistic and it's very difficult at the same time. We live in a hyper speed mode twenty-four hours, seven days a week. Our lives were much simpler before our "Hi-Tech helpers" wiped out our peace of mind and took away our downtime.

Let me explain in a little more detail. Think of our lives before the introduction of fax, e-mail, cell phones, computers, and the Internet. These are all wonderful tools to help us be more productive and to get things done and are combined with a promise for more personal time as the end result. What a great benefit! However, the real result is that we are expected to be "on" 24/7. An example is the growing number of what I call the "Crack Berry Addicts." These folks can't seem to turn off their BlackBerry devices. How in the world can these individuals stay focused on their list of priorities? The constant interruptions mean a constant change of their priorities and focus as the day progresses. This dramatically impacts their ability to get things done.

Wright

Tom, what you just described is valid. I can certainly relate. I am often guilty of what you describe. It seems terminal to our productivity. What is your response to those of us who really want to "fix" this situation? It there a solution that's truly workable?

Bay

The answer is a resounding yes—if we are committed. First recognize the issue at hand and be accountable to the most important person in your life—yourself. Second, take the responsibility to "fix it." David, notice my emphasis on accountability and responsibility. Here's my reasoning: If I don't recognize that I'm the only person to take care of myself then no one is taking care of me. No one else is responsible for my well being.

It's a very simple concept and yet so difficult to grasp, primarily because we are going at warp speed with our hair on fire trying to cope. In other words, we tend to form habits in dealing with priorities based on crisis, trauma, and urgency. This is certainly not a productive avenue to take for getting things done. It's all about changing directions. Almost everything we do is affected by an interruption—up, down, left, right, stop, go, back up, and go forward. David, how in the world are we going to end up at a final destination and achieve accomplishment or better yet, get things done?

Wright

Now we seem to be getting the core of the issue and maybe a focus on the resolution. If I'm right (no pun intended) what is the next step after I take responsibility to accept accountability for my results both positive and negative?

Bay

Okay, step one—managing your time and setting priorities. Keeping in mind that we have all the time there is—1,440 minutes, no more, no less, our productivity takes place in this timeframe, so management of our time is vital.

Wright

Tom, please excuse my interruption, but I need to address this for our audience. Many of our readers know you and your very direct remarks about "time management." You are often quoted saying that, "Time management is an oxymoron—a contradiction." In fact, I've heard you say, "We can't manage time." Will you please explain and clarify before we move on?

Bay

Yes, you are absolutely correct and thank you for that interruption. In fact, what's even more shocking is the fact that I taught time management classes for almost ten years for a premier company (the Franklin Quest Day Planner Organization). I still carry my Franklin Planner every day, everywhere, seven days a week. Now that *really* destroys my credibility! So let me explain.

We use the term "time management" constantly. We also have many different methods to try and manage our time. The following are some examples. Many people will move their clocks ahead ten, fifteen, or twenty minutes in their homes, offices, automobiles, etc. In many cases they don't move the time ahead the same amount to add a little more sense of anxiety or urgency. This way they really don't know the time for sure. They just know it's about right or approximate and it's ahead at some rate so they won't be late.

Just today before my interview with you, I had a pre-consult with a new client. She needs help getting organized and is underwater with her new business, which is very successful but things are starting to fall through the cracks—things like not being on time for appointments, forgetting appointments, not following up on her promises, late responses, and incomplete work, etc. Not the way to build a new and successful venture. She was explaining her plight to a mutual friend who told her "you need to talk to Tom Bay A.S.A.P.!"

She called me immediately and left a voice mail about her plight. I was very appreciative and returned her call within the hour to set up an appointment. I also left a short, to-the-point message on her voice mail. I stated that I could help her and that we needed two to three hours, perhaps over an extended lunch away from her normal chaos so we could focus on "getting things done." David, three days later I still hadn't heard from her, which, I might add, did not surprise me. I knew in my mind I would most likely have to call her again. So I called and left her messages three more times. The fourth time I got her "live" and in person. Jackpot!

Listen to her very first reaction: "Tom, thank you, thank you! I've had you on my call-back list for the past four days." No surprise. No wonder her success is taking a left turn and "heading south" very quickly and picking up speed. She is so busy bailing with a tea cup that she doesn't have time to stop and get a bucket. Do you get my drift?

Wright

Absolutely! So please continue. I want to hear where this is headed. We've all experienced your teacup/bucket analogy.

Bay

Well, here's my point. I started out asking her basic questions about how she prioritizes her day and manages her time. Listen to her immediate response: "Well Tom, I'm a little embarrassed to tell you this but each clock in my home and office is set ahead anywhere from ten to twenty minutes so I'm motivated to keep moving."

Gee, David, do you think I was surprised? Not in the least. Then she tells me she's going to buy a time system of some sort to help her get organized. I cautioned her not to buy anything until we met and discussed her overall needs. I told her we needed to talk about the big picture and not just the quick fix or take the band-aid approach. Then I asked, "Do you also move your watch ahead ten to fifteen minutes?

"Oh yes," she laughed, "my watch is always fifteen minutes ahead."

I chuckled and said, "Sally, you're smart and I'll guarantee you that every time you look at your watch you subtract the fifteen minutes and you're still late for most or all of your commitments."

There was a long pause. "Tom, you're right," she admitted.

We both laughed at our honesty. Then I made the statement that capsulized what this book is all about, the title says it all. "Sally, enough of this panic and stress. It's time to focus and start *getting things done!*"

Wright

So Tom, with this build-up, are you now going to share your formula with our listeners and readers?

Bay

Exactly. I call the formula "Laser Focus." I relate it to the force and the concentration of light and energy in a laser beam. Let me explain more clearly. A laser beam is a device containing gas or crystal and when stimulated by focused light waves, it can amplify and concentrate these waves, then emit them in a narrow, very intense beam. This beam can cut through steel like butter. The key words here, David, are "amplify" and "concentrate." This is the point I make with my clients and myself as well. We must concentrate our energy and focus to cut through all the "stuff" that gets in our way of being productive.

Wright

So with all the interruptions and chaos, how in the world can we concentrate much less amplify this concentration?

Bay

Great lead-in question, David. First, we must decide that it's important to accomplish the goal—nothing new here. Everything in life is based on choice. Most people stumble with making the choice. We live in such a victim society that most people don't make the choice and then blame the lack of productivity on someone other than themselves. I'm sure you've heard the remarks: "If it weren't for my boss," "My family is too demanding," "The guy at work just won't do his job," "I have to do my job and the job of my lazy co-worker," "If it weren't for my brother, sister, friend, wife, husband—" on and on. What is really being stated, David, is that, "It's not *my* fault that I'm not productive."

So step number one is to *step up!* Accept the responsibility to take control of your life. In fact, I start many of my speaking engagements with these questions: Whose life is it? Who's responsible for it? What do you plan on doing about it? And finally—when? If you are ready to answer all four questions honestly then you're ready to be productive and use your personal laser beam.

Step two is to activate a laser focus by looking at your values in life. Ask yourself: what do I really value in life? No one can answer that question for you. Taking the time to recognize your values will give you the drive and the desire to focus. I'm sure most people do have a value to be productive. With productivity comes a feeling of calm, less stress, better health, and a true sense of well being. In many cases this translates into success in all areas of one's life—personal and professional. As I've stated earlier, getting things done is one of the keys to a successful life.

Now, this point takes me to the core of what we call time management. As previously stated we don't manage time. We don't have control of time. It clicks off one second at a time. Time is a measurement of the events in our lives; it is how we can gauge our success or lack thereof. In two words it all comes down to *event control.*

Wright

So Tom, are you saying that it is event control that sets us apart from the term "time management"?

Bay

That's exactly what I'm stating. Event control is the answer to getting things done in all parts of our lives. Every day we have billions of events that take place. Everything is an event. Every step we take is an individual event. An example is just starting our day with the alarm clock going off. Setting the alarm, turning off the alarm, getting out of bed, dressing, eating breakfast, etc., all are events. Billions and billions of events occur during each twenty-four-hour period. Just the thought of this can be very overwhelming. It takes a very simple turn for the good when we realize that there are only two events we must deal with on a daily basis.

Wright

So after all this explanation of events, you're breaking it down to just two events?

Bay

Yes, two "types" or categories of events would be a better statement. The two categories of events are: events I control and events I don't control.

The events we control (or have the option to control because again, it's a choice). We must make pertaining to ourselves. Everything else is out of our control, it's very basic. Events that pertain to me I have the choice to control or not. All other events are out of my control—end of subject. So you can see why some people are so successful with their business and life in general. It's because they take control of their events; they also don't waste time or energy on things out of their control. Now when we take control of our events, we are activating the laser focus I referred to earlier.

The concentration of our energy is done by putting a list together and then giving this list a set of priorities. I use an A, B, C format:

A = must
B = should
C = could

There is no room for D—"D" stands for dump it! The priority list is the same as the intense beam given off by a laser. We become the personification of a laser beam when we cut through all the "stuff" and focus our energy and talent on what's truly important. Therefore, we can get things done and yield a high level of positive results. Note I said "positive results." Just having results is not the answer. Many times results can just be mediocre or even inferior.

Wright

That's an interesting statement. What draws you to that conclusion?

Bay

Here's how it works: Time is the same as money. When you make a financial investment or spend cash in some manner you will get a return on your investment of cash spent. If you buy a car, your return on your investment in the vehicle itself—the use of it, transportation mode, an ego boost, utility use, etc.—is a gain. There is also a secondary result. The cash spent cannot be spent on something else (e.g., a boat, house payment, flat-screen home theater system, clothing, etc.). All these things are called "opportunity cost." You can spend that cash once; everything that could have been purchased automatically becomes opportunity cost. If your opportunity cost is higher than your return on investment then you would have to ask if you had made a worthwhile investment.

David, it's exactly the same with time. When we invest time (event control) we have a return on our investment, and just as importantly, we will have many opportunity costs involved. The ideal situation is to obtain the highest return on investment while having lower opportunity costs. Asking that question when setting our priorities is a major step in getting things done. Looking at a list of let's say ten items, and using this criterion will really help in setting up the A, B, C format. The priorities in A should be the highest return, B the next highest, and so on.

Individuals using their laser focus and recognizing their highest return of time invested will always get things done in business, relationships, volunteerism, and in life over all.

Wright

Today we've been talking with Dr. Tom Bay, PhD and it has been very evident that he has a passion for his life and productivity. As stated earlier he has inspired thousands of individuals to look within or do without.

You are a man who walks his talk, Tom. Listening to you and reviewing all your past accomplishments proves your point about a laser thinking approach to life. It can be accomplished by anyone who makes the choice, as you so aptly put it. Thank you for your simple, yet in-depth explanation of how to get things done.

Tom, thank you for investing your time with us. I know that for myself and our readers, our return on investment will be very high.

Bay

Thank you. I'm humbled by your remarks. David, your quality interviews make it very easy for me to personally get a high return on my time invested. Thank you so much and I look forward to future interviews with you.

About the Author

For the past thirty-five years Dr. Tom Bay has been improving the productivity and morale of key executives of some of the most prominent businesses and organizations in the nation. He has appeared before all the Fortune 500 companies. His consulting company Tom Bay Speaks Up, Inc., located in Southern California, specializes in attitude makeover, as well as presentations on life management, team building, and employee productivity and morale.

Tom Bay, PhD
3027 McNab Avenue
Long Beach, CA 90808
E-mail: TomBay@TomBay.com

Chapter 8

KEITH HERNDON

THE INTERVIEW

David Wright (Wright)

Today we're talking with Keith Herndon. Keith is a consultant, writer, and speaker with extensive experience in the media and technology industries. He has excellent credentials in strategic planning and technology management. Prior to launching his consulting firm, Internet Decisions LLC, he was an executive with several companies including vice president of planning and product development at Cox Interactive Media, president of a business incubator, vice president and general manager of One Source Pro, and director of operations at Cox Radio Interactive. In his early career he was a business reporter and editor at the *Atlanta Journal-Constitution,* which established his skills as a writer and communicator.

He holds a bachelor's degree in journalism from the University of Georgia and a master's degree from the University of Oklahoma. Also, he completed a Davenport Fellowship at the University of Missouri.

Keith is active in several professional associations and is a Certified Seminar Leader as designated by the American Seminar Leaders Association.

Keith, welcome to *Getting Things Done*.

Keith Herndon (Herndon)

Thank you for having me here today.

Wright

So you began your career as a journalist and editor but transitioned into technology management. That's an interesting change. How did that come about?

Herndon

My career transition coincided with a period when the newspaper publishing industry was implementing significant technology changes. We were switching from the old mainframe publishing systems into client/server systems. Management was looking for someone who understood how the production processes worked from an editorial perspective so I volunteered to get involved in the technology transformation. In addition to retiring the old mainframes we got rid of all of the dark rooms as digital photography became cost effective.

As those projects were underway—we were in the middle of a complete digital transition—the Internet came along and presented all sorts of new opportunities and challenges for the media industry. I happened to be at the right place at the right time as the newspaper industry was exploring this new technology and trying to figure out how to implement it effectively.

Wright

The name of your company is Internet Decisions LLC. What does that mean exactly?

Herndon

The "Internet" part of the name represents the technology component of what we do. The "Decisions" part of the name is about helping businesses make the right decisions. Businesses put a lot of money, thought, and time into their technology decisions. Making the right decision is very important, but it can be challenging. We consider our company to be about providing business owners and managers with the tools, insight, and guidance that will help them make better decisions, especially when it comes to Internet strategies and other technology choices they have to make.

Wright

How do you think technology factors into the theme of *Getting Things Done?*

Herndon

I've always felt that businesses should look at technology as a productivity driver. From that perspective, technology should be all about helping you and your employees get things done. It's not about buying the latest gizmo or trying to install the latest software to impress the golfing buddies. It's important for managers to look at the needs of the business or the needs of their personal situation and adapt the technology to a problem that must be solved.

The way I look at this, and the way I try to get others to approach it, is that technology should be deployed to help you get things done.

Wright

Do you find that companies mix technology decisions with other business decisions? In other words, how do personnel and financial issues enter into decisions about technology?

Herndon

Personnel and financial implications are important considerations when making technology decisions. If someone is trying to sell a business manager a Windows-based system, but the company only has UNIX engineers to do support, there would be a problem. The business would have to factor in additional hiring or training. As for financial implications, companies must always look for solutions that fit a budget. The trend that is emerging, however, is that managers of all types are learning that they don't have to spend a lot of money to solve a simple problem. The open source software movement and innovations such as wiki-based collaboration tools and Internet telephony are making once very expensive solutions much more affordable. Internet telephony, also called VoIP (Voice over Internet Protocol), is one of the biggest innovations underway, allowing businesses to slash their telephone expenses.

There is so much new technology and innovation that allows small businesses as well as large enterprises to accomplish a lot with relatively little outlay as compared to ten years ago.

Wright

Is it possible to develop a needs analysis for companies that don't know exactly how to begin in e-business?

Herndon

It's important to first of all understand what is meant by the phrase "e-business" in that context. E-business doesn't necessarily mean that you're going to sell a physical product online. Companies that sell services can also be involved in e-business. Media companies, for example, can use e-business technologies to improve how they manage content even if a direct sale isn't involved. E-business also means deploying the Internet to help manage internal processes.

From that standpoint, any business can take advantage of e-business. Developing a needs analysis means taking a look at what your business does in the real world and mapping that into how it should work in a virtual world. It can be very eye-opening for businesses when leaders start trying to map their processes and translate them into an e-business environment. In many cases they discover they have tremendous inefficiency that can be improved through an e-business process.

Wright

Just how important are the right decisions when a business considers time saved and money invested?

Herndon

A business manager should look at the problem from multiple angles as part of the analysis: how will the decision affect my sales team, my customers, or my ability to deliver my product or service? Making the right decisions up front will prevent you from having to go back and reinvent something after you've already invested money.

There are many stories about owners of companies who fail to do their homework. They come away with something less than they could have gotten had they taken the time to research the options and make choices from a position of strength. There are business owners who spend more time on the type of car they will lease than on their technology vendor and then they wonder why things aren't working.

Wright

Every time I do something new I experience some initial fear. It's like I want to put my toe in the pool before I dive in. For those companies that are not involved presently in e-business, are there any logical steps to being successful? Can any business profit from e-business?

Herndon

Sure. Any business can take advantage of certain efficiencies that the Internet and technology in general can bring about.

For companies that are not necessarily involved in selling a physical product online, managers must look at the type of problem they are trying to solve. Then look at the types of technologies available to address that specific problem. Take a look at what other companies in the industry are doing. Look at what your customers are doing to solve a similar problem. Managers should address the task of buying technology from the perspective of solving a problem rather than a purchasing decision. The process should work in a way that when you make the decision, you feel reasonably comfortable that the problem will be solved. When you achieve this level of comfort, then you have a better feeling about the money you're spending. You can quantify a return on investment when you know that you're actually solving a problem.

Wright

You have stated that making the right decision often requires information that companies or individuals do not possess. What do you mean by that?

Herndon

Most company owners can't possibly know everything they need to know to make the right decisions. For example, they may not know what competitors are doing in a certain situation or in certain markets. They might not know all the various vendors who have products that could potentially solve the problem. In order to make the right decision, companies have to engage in research. Too often managers want to take the shortcut and pick something from a vendor they know or who may offer (or seems to offer) the best price up front without really having the full picture. When I say that making a right decision often requires information you don't possess, what I'm really saying is that to make a right decision means doing the necessary homework—to analyze the problem and study the solutions that are available.

Wright

What do you think is the most important aspect of creating a plan for using technology?

Herndon

The most important thing in deploying technology is to figure out which problem you're trying to solve. You have to understand that you're not buying technology for the sake of buying technology but that your business has certain needs and issues. Figure out what those needs and issues are and then look for the right technology to solve the problem as opposed to buying the technology and then trying to find problems for it to solve.

Wright

You say that researching potential vendors is an important part of the technology purchasing process—it will save time and money. Will you tell our readers a little bit more about that?

Herndon

A company's leaders may know they need to put in a new e-commerce system or upgrade the system they have because it may not be scaled properly. They should first identify the specific problem to be solved. They should then create a list of the various options available. That could entail talking with the company's competitors to find out what they're doing. It might mean talking with various vendors, looking at their Web sites and seeing who they have partnered with that may be familiar. It could involve conducting a thorough market analysis about various vendor solutions that would explain how other companies are solving the problem. Simply creating a matrix of vendors with such information as a brief product description, how much they're charging, and a list of client references can help bring the decision process into focus.

References are important. Companies will hire an employee and perform a thorough reference check. They will put ten times as much money into a software system or a technology platform, but will not call the first reference. It just doesn't make sense.

A lot of companies don't have the resources or the time to do the necessary research, so that's when they should consider using a research consultant to do it for them. A consultant can be their ears and eyes in the marketplace and talk with sources of information, such as a competitor that the company may not be able to reach on its own.

Wright

As you have been answering all these questions I'm getting this picture that if I should start a new business, the smart money would be spent on technology to check all kinds of sources about that business in particular, vendors, pricing—you could almost save yourself two to five years of getting this information by experience. Is that perception correct?

Herndon

Absolutely. The process I've talked about applies not only to a technology plan, but to the overall business plan as well. There is so much information available to businesses through the Internet as well as commercial databases that companies do not need to suffer from a lack of knowledge. Companies should take advantage of being able to search what their competitors are doing or what their potential competitors might be doing.

It would be foolhardy with so much information available to launch something without actually doing the homework and learning about the market. There is certainly enough data on the Internet; there's a tremendous amount of public information out there to build a credible business plan without spending a lot of money. It's just a matter of knowing where to go and knowing how to do the searches to find relevant information.

Wright

It seems that people are often afraid of making the leap into a technology decision because they think that once they commit to something it will quickly be obsolete. How can this way of thinking be overcome?

Herndon

Anytime you're dealing with technology you have to acknowledge the fact that once you buy something, there's going to be something else faster and sleeker and prettier on the market very soon after you close the deal. It's such a rapid development process now that companies can't worry about the obsolescence as much as they need to realize the consequences of what would happen if they don't make the investment in the needed technology. Will they be able to keep up with their competitors? Are they able to keep their employees as productive as they can be? These are the kinds of questions leaders should be asking when they make an investment in technology.

If they have made the right decision and spent an appropriate amount of money to solve a problem—as long as the problem stays solved—then they shouldn't worry too much about obsolescence. As markets evolve and the original problem evolves into something completely different, the technology may need an upgrade or it may be time to invest in different and new technology to take advantage of what it can offer.

Again, the key is to know that what you're buying solves the problem today and will likely solve the problem for the foreseeable future, and then be prepared to invest more capital as the situation evolves and needs change.

Wright

I had that same feeling for a long time but my practical experience indicates that things I thought would become obsolete were not obsolete—I didn't have to throw them away—almost everything I bought was upgradeable. If there wasn't enough memory in a computer I could buy more memory. Not knowing about technology, when people said it would become obsolete, to me that meant I would have to discard it. That's really not the case is it?

Herndon

People use the term "obsolete" when they really just want something fancier or newer. We often apply our love of the automobile to the way we approach technology. We want to get that new car every two to five years and that's probably true for the laptop computer we buy. We may use it for two years and then want a fancier more sleek one so we can compete with the guy sitting next to us on the airplane. So it's not always about obsolescence at all; it's about that desire to have the latest and greatest. Sometimes that's not the best decision to make. You have to make the tough calls in cases like those and know that when you're spending money on technology you're spending it for the right business reasons.

Wright

As we consider your approach, do business leaders/owners have the option of asking you to help them with making the hard decisions regarding technology?

Herndon

We engage with businesses in a number of different ways. We work with businesses when they understand they do not have all the information necessary to make a decision—that they need to have someone come in and help them do additional research on the problem and available solutions. We help managers when they need documentation to explain choices to others; we conduct strategic planning sessions to help businesses identify problems and potential solutions.

It's really about assisting with and enabling the decision process, and we can engage at any step along that process.

Wright

Using technology always means change. How would you suggest that managers break it to their people, especially those who don't want to change? How do managers introduce technology so that it will be embraced rather than being protested?

Herndon

One of the biggest mistakes that companies of all sizes make is that they don't consider the investment that must be made in employee training. That's a very, very big issue for a lot of companies. They will budget a project and then they'll realize it will be too complicated for their people to learn on their own. And there is no money left for training.

Business owners and managers must understand that when they make any type of a decision regarding technology there has to be consideration given to how it's going to be used within the organization. Having a communication plan and having a training plan is important. Also important is the timing of introducing a new technology. For example, if you are a retail store and you're going to go online, no one should ever recommend doing that in November or December.

Wright

What an interesting conversation, Keith. I really appreciate your taking this time to discuss something that is extremely important to the American businessperson.

Herndon

I appreciate being asked to participate in this project, David.

Wright

Today we've been talking with Keith Herndon. He is a consultant and writer. He's a speaker with extensive experience in the media and technology industries. As we have found out here, I think he knows what he's talking about, at least I'm going to take his advice.

Keith, thank you so much for being with us today on *Getting Things Done.*

About the Author

KEITH L. HERNDON is a consultant, writer, and speaker with extensive experience in the media and technology industries. He has credentials in strategic planning and technology management. Prior to launching his consulting firm, Internet Decisions LLC, he was an executive with several companies including Vice President of Planning and Product Development at Cox Interactive Media, President of a business incubator, Vice President and General Manager of One Source Pro, and Director of Operations at Cox Radio Interactive. In his early career, Keith was a business reporter and editor at *The Atlanta Journal-Constitution,* which established his skills as a writer and communicator. He holds a bachelor's degree in journalism from the University of Georgia and a master's degree from the University of Oklahoma. He also completed a Davenport Fellowship at the University of Missouri. Keith is active in several professional associations and is a Certified Seminar Leader as designated by the American Seminar Leaders Association.

Keith L. Herndon
2514 Brookdale Drive
Atlanta, GA 30345
E-mail: keith@internetdecisions.com
www.internetdecisions.com

Chapter 9

DR. GABRIELA CORÁ

David Wright (Wright)

Today we're talking with Dr. Gabriela Corá. Dr. Corá is president of the Executive Health and Wealth Institute, Inc., an international consulting firm assisting executives and corporations in individual and organizational health and wealth. Her extensive expertise in crisis leadership inspired her to design a powerful program assisting executives in "leading under pressure," providing for effective strategies to maximize peak performance and productivity while maximizing health and well-being. Her energized enthusiasm, strategic focus, and innovative style are qualities in action as an expert consultant, executive coach, information entrepreneur, and professional speaker, making her a key collaborator of Fortune 500 corporations and international organizations, including The Coca-Cola Company, The Pharmaceutical Industry, The Cleveland Clinic Foundation, The World Bank, and The Entrepreneurs' Organization. Dr. Corá is a licensed medical doctor, mediator, and she has a master's in business administration.

Dr. Corá, what is "life-work balance"?

Dr. Gabriela Corá (Corá)

Life-work balance is a myth. It's a nice way of trying to make some sense out of our very busy lives by attempting to "do it all" and all at the same time. We are basically "supposed" to be busy, effective, and productive in our lives, including in our everyday activities, caring for our personal needs, as well as productive in our professional careers. It is not a matter of either/or, balancing how much of our time is spent here or there (i.e., working, exercising, having a meal, spending time with family and friends). It's more about integrating effective ways of working well, living well, and joyfully. I believe the key is to effectively manage work in life.

Wright

That's better explained than I've ever heard it. How does the corporate executive or entrepreneur currently manage life and work?

Corá

Well, what I've seen in my practice as a doctor and in my work as a business coach of corporate executives and entrepreneurs is that many are managing their lives with difficulty. They're basically putting so much time into their work activities that their personal needs are not necessarily met. I find that many executives give priority to work-related matters and as a result they tend to disregard some of their biological and personal needs that provide the stamina they need not only to be creative and productive, but also to do very well in expanding their job opportunities.

Wright

So are you saying that some people put so much time into their work that they neglect their personal life and as a result they're not as good at work?

Corá

That's absolutely right. Many people believe that the more time they put into their work, the more productive they're going to be and the more results they're going to see. But if you're really exhausted, you lose your creativity and your ability to resolve matters in a faster, more efficient and effective way.

Have you ever experienced this problem: You may have been sitting at your computer for many hours and you notice you're getting stuck on a specific computer program. You're going one way and then another to try and fix it. You get so wrapped up in trying to resolve the problem that you spend a full hour on it and you end up frustrated, feeling that you just can't deal with it any longer. You take a break and after awhile, you come back refreshed. In a couple of minutes, you fix what you had been struggling with for an hour.

Wright

Yes, I had that experience last night, except I was dumb enough to spend three hours fighting with the program that, after a night's rest, I fixed in about ten minutes this morning.

Corá

That's what happens when our systems get exhausted and we get so hyper focused on a problem that we forget the big picture. Sometimes when we are more refreshed, it's easier for us not only to be more creative, but to fix and resolve issues in a better and more efficient way.

This makes up a lot of what I see in my work. As a doctor, I've been asked to provide medications (usually stimulants) so that people can either work sixteen-hour days or more, and/or stay at the office overnight without any sleep. This is not the best way to go. There is a biological reason for sleep: it allows us to recover our energy so that we're more effective throughout the course of the day. Sleep is one of the elements that allows us to be more productive, more creative, providing for a better ability for us to continue to grow our business.

Wright

I've known people who have searched for stimulants over the years so that they can work harder. I didn't realize they went to their doctors and asked for them too.

Corá

The use of stimulants may be more to the extreme. What people usually do is use stimulants that are readily available over the counter, or use culturally acceptable stimulants like caffeinated drinks. I see many successful professionals, executives, and entrepreneurs pumping up on coffee throughout the day to be effective. Then they will drink more and more alcohol at night because they cannot fall asleep. This is one of the problematic cycles I see: people are trapped into drinking more and more alcohol at night because they can't fall asleep. To wake up the next morning, they'll drink a lot of coffee and energy drinks during the day. They've now fallen into the cycle of using common stimulants like caffeine throughout the course of the day and alcohol and/or a sleep medication to sleep at night. If you look at it from a broad perspective, common sense will indicate that there's something wrong with that picture.

There are healthier ways in which we can maximize our energy and improve our productivity, and at the same time make sure that we take good care of ourselves.

Wright
What does the ideal world look like?

Corá
In the ideal world, we would be awake, working and/or studying for about eight hours and we would probably have pleasurable and recreational activities for another eight hours over the course of a single day. We would then sleep about eight hours every night. The ideal world is probably the healthiest standard but how many of us live in this ideal world?

The real world looks more like a place in which people are working anywhere from twelve to sixteen-hour days. The extra hours have to come from somewhere and usually the recreational activity part of the day is the first one to go. When people realize that they want to start working more to continue to be as efficient or make the same amount of money, or make more money than they were making before, they will start taking the necessary extra time from the pleasurable activities and add them into their work day. If that's not enough, they will start sleeping less. For busy executives or for successful entrepreneurs, the real world looks like sixteen-hour work-days, with maybe one or two hours of pleasurable activities and maybe five or six hours of sleep.

Wright
What are the key areas of your plan that you consider in order to effectively manage life and work?

Corá
To get things done, it is essential to look at the following areas to effectively manage life and work for our personal, professional, and organizational well-being:

- From an individual perspective, one of the most obvious and important areas is the physical dimension. Nutrition, sleep, exercise, and relaxation practices are the biological pillars of this area. This is where the mission that we have designed for ourselves manifests on the physical plane.
- Next is the emotional dimension. This is the area where our ability to connect with others resides. Our relationships with family and friends make our affective world rich and joyful.
- Our cognitive or intellectual dimension is next. In this area there is training, education, and the constant learning skills from a mental perspective. This is the area where our vision for the future is created.
- The next area has to do with social life and behavior. As a person, our well-being and growth also depends on our ability to connect and inter-relate with our community, our work organization, and other organizations and cultures.
- Lastly is the spiritual dimension, which includes our relationship with a higher being or connection with our higher self through prayer, meditation, and self-awareness. This area includes voluntarism, altruism, and esthetics. This is the key area where our values reside. Our individual ethics connect to our value system within this area.

All of these dimensions are essential components of the healthy lifestyle and interact in dynamic processes.

Productivity and performance processes operate within each of these areas, allowing us to constantly improve within each dimension. The above descriptions apply to a personal or individual perspective, but we can use the same framework in regards to a healthy organization.

Within the physical dimension I would include the safety, the structure, and the human element we choose for our organization, whether it's our own company or a multinational corporation. This is also where the organizational mission-in-action is brought to life.

The emotional dimension of a healthy organization includes the corporate culture—openness and trust, the ability to receive feedback, and sustain employee hope during critical times.

The intellectual dimension within an organization includes the training, the learning, and the skills training necessary to constantly improve within the organization. This is where the vision for the organization is created.

The social dimension includes the community involvement of an organization and the relationship that it creates with other corporations, cultures, and organizations.

In the spiritual dimension, the healthy organization's values compose the foundation of the organization. Ethical values, voluntarism, and altruism are key components within this area at the organizational level.

As in the individual healthy lifestyle, all of these dimensions are intimately related and interact in dynamic processes.

Performance and productivity within each dimension bring in the dynamic processes within each area, providing for the opportunity for constant improvement.

Wright

If I understand you correctly, you're saying that there are five key areas: physical, emotional, cognitive, social, and spiritual.

Corá

Yes, both from an individual as well as from an organizational perspective. The more aligned the individual dimensions are with the corresponding organizational dimensions, the better the relationship between the individual and his or her organization. The better alignment there is, the better the match, the better the chances of maximum productivity, performance, and longstanding well-being.

Wright

That leaves me wondering: what are the most common pitfalls you find in your work with coaching clients?

Corá

The most common pitfalls I've observed include the following: first, people putting too much emphasis on "must-do" activities, when in fact, they have an option to do or not do them. By creating a deadline too close to the present time, instead of allowing more flexibility, people just add too much (unnecessary) pressure upon themselves.

Second: keeping busy without a plan. I've worked with successful entrepreneurs and executives who have kept a very busy calendar. If you look at it with a fine eye, they have scheduled one activity after another without an overall plan or goal. There are many actions and reactions, but there is not necessarily a supporting backbone—no consistent strategy of why all these activities should take place. Often times, I find myself assisting others in creating priorities in businesses in which I have no expertise—to my clients' disbelief! However, the critical thinking process is universal, and the transferable skills are key to getting things done.

A third pitfall I've observed is people setting up "impossible" expectations. On a personal health level, this includes people wanting to lose ten pounds within a week, or wanting to exercise an hour and a half every day when they have not exercised for ten years. Unfortunately, unscrupulous businesses promote "miracle cures," feeding into the public demand. From a work perspective, people may want to make a million dollars within a month when they haven't even made a million dollars within a year. By creating these false expectations they are only setting themselves up for failure.

It is much easier to take smaller steps and create a more manageable set of goals so that we can not only meet those deadlines but also be successful in reaching each and every one of the successive levels until we are ready to take bigger steps.

For example, if you are interested in setting an exercise schedule, instead of starting off with an hour of exercise a day, you might start out with five minutes a day because that is a realistic goal. The following week, you may increase the time to ten minutes a day. People usually think this is too trivial or childish, when in fact it's more about making sure that you will succeed at reaching those step-by-step goals. At work, this may mean cutting down on endless meetings and re-structuring them into one-hour meetings with a beginning, middle, and end with clear deadlines and actions to follow.

Another pitfall I have observed with entrepreneurs and corporate executives in the area of entrepreneurial initiatives is they may find that a new and great idea may be exciting and dreadful at the same time since after all, the new idea will only take a life of its own. Many run after another great idea that may or may not be aligned with the overall plan. Sometimes it's harder to let go of an incredible opportunity rather than pursue it. After all, there are only twenty-four hours within the course of the day and we are the only ones who can choose wisely how to use our own time to bring joy into our lives and our families' lives.

Wright

Many people identify with these pitfalls but on the flip side, what are the most effective strategies you've found as you assist your clients?

Corá

The most effective strategies I've found in my consulting and executive coaching practice include the ability to conceptualize, think, and plan ahead of the game before actually going into action. This simple task provides the opportunity to find the best and shortest way to reach our goals. In an efficient system, instead of going through five steps, we can instead bypass one or two steps and just go straight to the next one. If we allow ourselves to observe the situation from a more global perspective, we can see which steps we can or cannot skip to achieve our goals.

If we want to go from point A to E, I would suggest that people look into the positives (pros) or negatives (cons) of going through each step first. This will help prioritize needs and wants. Once this has been decided, it is then appropriate to establish a path toward reaching our well thought-out goals.

SMART goals, first described by Locke and Latham in their motivational theory and modified over time with practical add-ons, include the need for goals to be specific, measurable, motivating, attainable, realistic, relevant, tangible, and trackable through time. We can easily apply this strategic approach in improving and achieving a higher level in our work performance and productivity, as well as in our health and well-being.

For example, if we want to relax via physical activity, we would schedule a plan containing a repetitive exercise, such as using a treadmill or cycling. Repetitive (and usually boring) exercises are best at providing a relaxed, meditative-like state. We would start with five minutes daily the first week, increasing to ten minutes the following week and so on until reaching a desired thirty minutes per day, as suggested by the American Medical Association.

To simplify the overall strategy, I have designed and implemented the following concepts both in my coaching as well as in my medical practice. I call it "AIM I AM," and I use this acronym in a constant improvement cycle. "AIM" stands for Align, Integrate, and Manage your plan. "I AM" stands for Improve, Achieve, and Maintain each targeted goal.

Let's address the "I AM" component. Once again, "I" stands for Improve, "A" stands for Achieve, and "M" stands for Maintain. If I want to improve a specific area—let's say that I am over-scheduling, my very busy calendar overflows and I want to improve this—I would start by prioritizing the demands, making sure that every activity is aligned and integrated with my overall plan and then I would implement specific actions that I want to accomplish. So, I would *Improve* the issue to be resolved, *Achieve* the goal, and then *Maintain* that desired goal before going on to the next level. It is key to Maintain; a common pitfall is to go, go, go, without testing the effectiveness of the intervention. After this, repeat the cycle: Improve, Achieve, and Maintain your goal.

One of the problems I've observed is that many people want to constantly improve, but they don't stop for a minute to contemplate their success. Some may obtain a huge victory but may not enjoy their accomplishment for even a split second. They are living in the future and working on the next task, rather than grounding themselves in their present. Taking some time in the "here and now" after achieving a goal is essential for the experience of joy and well-being.

The next area to consider is also part of the "AIM I AM" strategy. As mentioned, "AIM" stands for Align, Integrate, and Manage individual and organizational plans. Through years of coaching clients, mentoring colleagues and employees, and helping patients, I have realized that the more people are deeply aligned on a personal and professional level, the happier and more effective they are in their lives. For example, exercise time and meal times need to be added as daily entries to become an integral part of routine activities. All networking activities should be aligned and integrated with underlying strategy, and be consistent with the overall plan. By aligning your goals, you are bringing consistency to your plan. Recreational activities should be added as well. Whatever does not fall within the plan should be discarded.

For example, if you have left a specific activity on the back burner for two years, you might as well delete it from your list. If you decide it should be a priority, then you should schedule it now.

The Managing component is a very dynamic process. Your plan should be tested at specific intervals and should not be carved in stone. Instead, its purpose is to provide for a tangible opportunity for improvement.

Wright

I am fascinated by your wealth of knowledge on this subject of life and work management. How did you become an expert in this area?

Corá

I must admit, I became an expert in this area somewhat by default. In my practice as a medical doctor, my expertise is in psychiatry, specifically in mood and anxiety disorders. As a physician, I have seen many entrepreneurs and very busy executives who came in to see me once they were burnt out, depleted of energy, and with several medical issues at stake; sometimes with full-blown panic attacks, medical problems, and/or depression. Even if they had accumulated large, extensive wealth, they were not happy. Some of the medical issues that came up included not one but several visits to the emergency room fearing a heart attack. After a full check-up, with perfect diagnostic tests and healthy hearts, the emergency room doctors may have implied that a visit to the psychiatrist might be helpful.

Because of the stigma of potentially being diagnosed with a mental illness or seeing a counselor, many people decided not to visit the psychiatrist, saying, "This can't be. These symptoms are so real, so physical, and there's no way that there could be anything else going on."

I realized that there was a need that the medical system was not able to fully address in an effective way. Additionally, back in the nineties, I had become very interested in the business component as well, by coaching, advising, and consulting at the corporate level. My father is a successful entrepreneur, and my mother always worked in international organizations. I was born with an entrepreneurial spirit and also grew up in a business environment. The paradigm of effectively integrating health and wealth strategies was uncharted territory and I saw a tremendous opportunity in putting it all together. This amazing challenge is what motivated and inspired me to create the Executive Health and Wealth Institute, Inc.

As I started sharing my ideas, knowledge, and experience with this integrative approach, speaking at national and international events, working more with corporate executives and entrepreneurs, people started to ask me, "You talk about leading under pressure and life-work management, do you practice what you preach?" As a psychiatrist, my training involved a zealous protection of my privacy: I would disclose personal information only if it benefited my client or patient. This was a turning point in deciding to share my own experiences.

Managing work in life has been a key factor in my personal and professional success. I graduated as a medical doctor with honors at twenty-four with two babies—one was two years old and the other was just nine months old. I always considered my family's well-being a priority. I grew up as a professional practicing doctor, very interested in the business interface, and actively managing life and work on a regular basis. I have had very busy schedules, particularly during training time, and have always ensured that I did very well in each and every aspect of my life. I believe I became an expert in this area because of my training in the science, theory, and practice as well as having experienced and managed these challenges myself.

Wright

That is very impressive to have graduated with a doctorate at twenty-four and to have two children.

Corá

Thank you. I studied hard, slept very little and juggled activities addressing everybody's needs to the best of my ability. I would sometimes work throughout the night so that I could be with my children and family during the day. Many of the ideas and suggestions I propose are not just theory—I have successfully implemented these strategies as a coach, as a doctor, as a mentor, as a boss, and I have found them helpful in managing my own work in life.

My time is spent with my family, with my friends, in my part-time practice as a doctor, and in my full-time practice as a corporate consultant, speaker, and coach in the United States and around the world.

Wright

Going back a little bit, you said there's a stigma about consulting with a psychiatrist. It is unfortunate that we as a population aren't more educated. We don't think anything of going to the doctor if we sprain our ankle but if we "sprain" our mind it's almost considered shameful to go to a psychiatrist.

Corá

You are right, David. It's so much easier to attribute a problem to the physical world, have a headache and point to the head, or complain of a stomachache and attribute the problem to something we ate. It's hard to identify the physical location for sadness or extreme anxiety, although we now know the brain location and processes behind these medical symptoms.

It's much more difficult to explain why someone who may "have it all" is depressed. We try to make sense of the way we understand the world—we try to make sure that there is some rational reason for everything and we fear anything that we cannot control. Stigmatizing psychiatric help has played a significant role and is probably one of the reasons why many executives don't seek help earlier. Another reason is they don't prioritize their own needs. As corporate executives and entrepreneurs are constantly leading under pressure, it's easier to say they're stressed out than to say they're having full-blown panic attacks. The intervention is different in either case, requiring a specific strategic approach for its successful resolution.

For example, I like to discuss stress and well-being as a continuum. There can be stress and well-being at the same time. Stress can be a wonderful source of stamina and the fuel that motivates us to improve. Stress can help us and can be beneficial. But too much stress can cause tiredness, burnout, exhaustion, or disease—the absence of well-being. When there is disease, it's essential to resolve it on a biological level. The longer a person is ill, the longer it will take that person to fully recover.

Executive coaching can be very helpful if someone feels somewhat disorganized or has difficulty prioritizing needs. However, when people are clinically depressed, they may not be able to see all the options in their lives and work-lives and less so the full spectrum of opportunities. They may feel stuck on the issues to be resolved because their resilience—their ability to bounce back—may have been exhausted. It is imperative for busy executives to maximize their biological output in a healthy way. They must master and maximize the effectiveness of the four pillars of biological well-being: sleep, nutrition, exercise, and relaxation. Creating a healthy baseline will allow them to effectively lead under pressure. If their system has already been exhausted though, they will need to seek help from a healthcare professional to repair the problem before they can continue to improve at work. An individual's health is a priority.

I see many executives who are more ready to prioritize their business needs over their biological ones and often end up ignoring their biological needs until they are sick. As a result, although they may have a tremendous amount of stamina when they are well and work like three people instead of one, they may be sick for a full month after they've completely exhausted themselves. My wish is for people to better understand how they can help themselves at each and every level of their work-life and personal life to live the most successful and joyful life that they can.

My strategy in consulting executives, entrepreneurs, and their organizations, is to "speak" the business language, applying business coaching and health-related strategies. My formal biological psychiatry research training provided for an excellent foundation with the consistent use of scientific methodology and the practical experience of having evaluated, diagnosed, treated, coached, and intervened at all stages of health and disease. Add my business training and corporate experience to the integration of health and wealth strategies and all of these become the key elements of my toolbox.

Wright

If you could look into the future, what do you anticipate will happen in the life of the busy executive or entrepreneur?

Corá

I believe many women have looked into integrating effective strategies as they have forced themselves into the workforce while juggling everything for their families. On the other hand, many career women have decided against building a family in order to devote themselves to their work.

Not as many men decide against having a family to pursue their professional careers. In the future, there may be even more women shifting from high-paying corporate jobs into entrepreneurial opportunities with the idea that this will enable them to maintain some control and independence as they manage life and work. Men are getting closer though, particularly as many men feel that working 24/7 and not spending enough time with their family and friends takes away joy from their lives. Some men are choosing not to work as many hours and make less money to be sure they can enjoy their wealth in a different way.

More women in the corporate and business world have decided to reduce their work hours to spend more time with their family. Interestingly, many of these women who have chosen to work on a part-time basis are still working forty plus hours a week whereas their male counterparts work sixty plus hour weeks. More men wonder about potential alternative ways of rearranging their lives, work responsibilities, and recreational activities.

I foresee many "rebelling" against corporate cultures that demand absolute devotion. Instead, many will choose to take more time to enjoy themselves, whether it is through sports, travel, and/or stimulating activities, including every life dimension: physical, emotional, and intellectual. People may focus on family activities rather than just spending some fun time on their own. I see some executives and entrepreneurs choosing to *not* stay an extra day away on business, even if they can have fun. Instead, many are choosing to spend their own money and bring their family along to spend some quality time together.

I foresee that people will work even more efficiently, prioritizing to the max, eventually working fewer hours and hopefully becoming even more productive. This is one of the first interventions that puzzle many as we start working together. Many doubt that they will be more productive, more relaxed, more in control, and feeling better, by reducing their work hours from sixteen to say, twelve; when they do, just a few weeks later they are in complete amazement. The bottom line is: finding alternative ways when someone has exhausted his or her resources is essential. At that stage it is vital to plan, reprioritize, and try new strategies for success.

Wright

Dr. Corá, is there anything else you'd like to add?

Corá

I would like to stress how important it is to have an overall plan. This plan does not take away the spontaneity that makes life interesting and exciting. Instead, it provides for a wonderful path to continue to improve within each area of our lives. The more capable the individual is at integrating, aligning, and managing the personal along with the organizational plan, the more successful he or she will be over time.

Work is a part of our productive lives; therefore, the need to manage work *is* part of life. Planning ahead allows us to keep responsibilities, needs, and wants in perspective. As we go through our plan, we may realize the need to shift gears or implement some changes. Even if they are challenging, these changes will allow us to achieve our ultimate goal. In this case, having a plan does not necessarily mean it will be easy to carry out what needs to be done. It will only enable us to foresee some potential pitfalls and avoid them beforehand.

As we masterfully design the turn-key to effectively managing work and life, and the more excited and passionate we become about our professional and career choices, the greater our ability to integrate a cohesive and comprehensive plan will be. Having fun at work and having fun doing what we do for a living adds pleasurable activities into our busy schedules. Those who work long hours because they enjoy their work so much will hopefully add some other recreational activities to the mix and continue to enjoy work and life. The ultimate goal needs to be clearly written in our vision statement, to achieve joy and well-being in every aspect of our lives.

About the Author

DR. CORÁ is President of The Executive Health & Wealth Institute, Inc., an international consulting firm based in Miami, Florida. Her expertise in crisis leadership inspired her to design a powerful program assisting executives in Leading under Pressure®, providing for effective strategies to maximize peak performance and productivity while maximizing health and well-being. Her energized enthusiasm, strategic focus, and innovative style are qualities in action as an expert consultant, executive coach, and speaker, making her a key collaborator of Fortune 500 corporations and international organizations. She is a licensed medical doctor, mediator, and has a master's in business administration.

Gabriela Corá, MD, MBA, President
The Executive Health & Wealth Institute, Inc.
Phone: 305.762.7632
Toll Free: 866.762.7632
www.ExecutiveHealthWealth.com

Chapter 10

BRIAN BIRO

David Wright (Wright)

Today we're talking with Brian Biro, "America's Breakthrough Coach." Brian is one of the nation's foremost speakers and teachers of leadership, possibility-thinking, thriving on change, teambuilding, and getting things done. Brian is author of the acclaimed bestseller, *Beyond Success,* and five other life-changing books. He was rated number one from over forty speakers at four consecutive *Inc* magazine international conferences. With degrees from Stanford University and UCLA, Brian has appeared on *Good Morning America,* CNN's *Business as Usual,* and *Fox News.*

Brian, welcome to *Getting Things Done.*

Brian Biro (Biro)

David, it's a pleasure being with you and I really enjoy this opportunity.

Wright

So you've written six books and traveled around the world speaking and teaching about teambuilding, leadership, life balance, thriving on change, and getting things done. What in your background prepared you to do this important work?

Biro

I think, David, the key thing is that I've always recognized that whatever it is that we do, it's about people. I had a background as an athletic coach and even though I coached swimming, what I really coached was people—my work has always been about helping people discover what is really inside of them and get closer to their full potential.

My friend and mentor, John Wooden, the great UCLA basketball coach, often said that there are no overachievers. I think, when it comes to getting things done, we sometimes forget that there is so much potential inside of us. The real joy and opportunity in life is to help people discover that true potential.

I began my career in athletics. Then I moved into the corporate world and I found out the same things that were important in working with athletes at a high level were also important in the business world. Success was really about teamwork and everyone understanding that we are all leaders in certain situations and times. Ultimately, we are the CEOs of our own lives. When you grab hold of personal responsibility it's amazing what kinds of things you'll accomplish because you simply won't allow them to remain undone.

Over the last sixteen years, as a professional speaker and writer, I've had the great opportunity of working with hundreds of different companies from virtually every industry. I've had the chance to see which organizations seem to have that special ability to climb to the top and stay there, to get things done, and to create an environment and culture that absolutely thrives on change.

There are some powerful common elements in these organizations. Number one, they have fun. It's so important to have fun; that's a tremendously important and productive corporate goal. They have enculturated the understanding that if you want to truly excel, you must move beyond merely respecting one another and go to the next level where you build genuine eagerness about working together. Moving from silos to synergy is a real key to moving from good to great.

Wright

In your bestselling book, *Beyond Success*, and in your seminars, you suggest that what we focus on is what we create. Will you give our readers a tip on how to use this understanding to help accelerate their performance and spirit?

Biro

That is such a powerful principle to build from. In my seminars I actually have people perform a physical experience where they reach around as far as they can and mark that spot visually. Then I have them do it again after they've envisioned going three feet farther. Whenever we do the exercise everyone in the room gasps because they thought they had stretched themselves to their ultimate limits. But simply by erasing the former vision of their possibilities and clearly seeing themselves going farther, they create a powerful new result.

Many of us have heard the statement, "What you focus on is what you get." But I've always felt that that was a little incomplete because you don't get anything if you don't really grab hold of personal responsibility. When you become fully engaged as a breakthrough leader, what you focus on is what you create. It takes your active participation to move your future in the direction you want it to go.

How often do you spend your time focusing on trying to avoid what you don't want rather than clearly envisioning what you do want? That choice of focus makes the difference between staying where you've been or moving to where you really want to be.

Wright

You have stated before that all of us are leaders. Most of us have been raised to think that there are a few leaders and a whole lot of followers. Will you tell us about your different view on leadership?

Biro

I'm called "America's Breakthrough Coach" because I believe we are born to be breakthrough leaders. We're all in the breakthrough business. For example, parenting is in the breakthrough leadership business! Every day is a breakthrough opportunity for parents. I call it a WOO—a Window Of Opportunity. We must break through with our kids so that they learn to make great decisions to keep them from moving in the direction of drugs or destructive kinds of choices and instead, build confidence and faith. Every single business meeting, retreat, or convention is a breakthrough opportunity for that organization. They hold those meetings to move to the next level of teamwork, results, and cultural excellence.

Breakthrough Leadership is built from a foundation of belief that we are self-leaders first and foremost. When you think about it, what is leadership? Leadership is simply making decisions. Any time you make a decision that's an act of leadership. It's clear with that definition that we are leaders and we are affecting other people every day by the way we conduct ourselves and deal with success, routine, and adversity. Some people recognize that within every adversity is planted the seed of an equivalent or greater benefit. And yet other people focus so much on adversity that the potential benefits and learning opportunities are rendered invisible. Remember, what you focus on is what you create. In everything we do we are always creating some example for someone—the people we work with, our families, and ultimately ourselves.

So when you come from a perspective that you are the CEO of your own life, you look at your life a little bit differently; you recognize that you do have choices and these choices affect others. The only thing that we don't have a choice about is that we're going to die; everything else is a matter of choice. When coming from that perspective, the great WOO is to go after life with a passion that you can create great things for others and yourself, you can get more done than you ever dreamed of, and that who you are does make a difference.

Wright

As America's Breakthrough Coach you're well-known for having participants in your events break through a one-inch thick wooden board as a personal breakthrough experience, which is an incredible team event. Will you tell us about that?

Biro

I'd love to. Even though I've led board-breaking over eleven hundred times, I can't wait to do it with the next group. The board-breaking experience serves as a tremendous metaphor for breakthroughs we want to make in our lives—to move beyond limits, obstacles, habits, or doubts that hold us back. Ultimately the only thing that does hold us back is some form of fear. The board-breaking experience is such a wonderful experience because people who have had no martial arts training accomplish something they didn't know they could do. I've had eighty-five-year-olds break boards. I've had seven-year-olds break boards. I've also had great big strong people not break the board at first because they thought it was about muscle and force. It's not—it's about what you focus on.

In the board-breaking experience everyone writes on the board a limit, obstacle, habit, or doubt that he or she wants to break through. Some examples of these obstacles could be: procrastination, stress, anger, imbalance, not enough time, or fear of failure. The people envision what the limit or fear has cost them up until now in their life. On the other side of the board they write down what's waiting for them as soon as they've broken through those obstacles. For example: joy, peace of mind, energy, or confidence. The team cheers exuberantly for each individual and joyfully celebrates each breakthrough.

The beauty of the board-breaking experience is that it's an on-target representation of what we have to face every day. We don't know what's coming today. We may have a pretty good idea but the actual truth is that each day holds the possibility of surprise. We're all in the business of breaking through that uncertainty. When you stand in front of that board for the first time you may be confident you can do it, you may have a very strong sense that you have what it takes to do it, but you've never actually done it before.

What I love about the board-breaking experience as an example of getting things done is that it's exactly what we face in our businesses every day. We're constantly challenged to do things we've never done before. Maybe the new challenges are very different from anything we've tackled before, or maybe they're just a little bit different. Building confidence through the board-breaking experience helps develop an attitude of, "Wow, I stood in front of that barrier and I didn't know I could do it. But when I went through it, it felt like a piece of paper!" The most important ingredient in breaking the board is the same one we talked about earlier—it's focusing not on the obstacle but on the breakthrough.

Wright

At the heart of your work are the three breakthrough tools. Will you tell our readers what these are and how they help us create breakthroughs?

Biro

The three breakthrough tools are: vision, personal responsibility, and the power of team.

Vision

All breakthroughs start with a vision.

I love to tell a story about a wonderful lesson my younger daughter, Jenna, taught me when she was four years old. (It's amazing how wise young children are!) At that time we lived in Hamilton, Montana, out where the movie, *A River Runs Through It*, took place.

One afternoon in late summer my wife, my two daughters, and I decided to go out to eat at our favorite café right in the heart of our little town. The café was on the second floor of an old Main Street brick building. As soon as we walked into the café it was immediately clear that everyone there had carved out their safe space—their haven, their comfort zone—called their table. Though you couldn't see them, there were unmistakable invisible barriers separating every table and keeping everyone at the comfortable arms-length distance. I call it polite co-existence. Like everyone else we quickly set up our comfort zone and our own invisible barriers as we quietly began talking about our day.

We often have those same invisible barriers separating our own teams within organizations like the walls that are sometimes built between sales, operations, and administration.

After about five minutes (because a four-year-old can't sit still for longer than that), Jenna got up and walked over to the windows. The most striking thing about this café was its windows. It had huge panoramic picture windows that looked at two unbelievably magnificent mountain ranges on either side of our narrow Bitteroot Valley. It was an absolutely breath-taking sight. But nobody saw it except Jenna. So engrossed was I in studying my menu, I hadn't noticed that Jenna had strayed away. When I finally looked up, I had a moment of panic when I thought, "Where's my little girl?"

Just then I spotted her at the window and breathed a sigh of relief. But just after I saw her, she whipped around toward us. As soon as I saw her little four-year-old face, I knew that everyone in that restaurant was in for a heap of trouble! You see, my little girl, though very small for four, was blessed with a very powerful set of lungs. With unstoppable excitement she instantly shattered the quiet atmosphere in the café by shouting out at the very top of her lungs, "Look, Mommy, Daddy, Kelsey, we're in heaven!"

Immediately the whole place went dead quiet. Everyone stared at us and we began to turn bright red. Meanwhile, Jenna was grinning ear to ear. After a moment or two of uncomfortable silence, the magic of the breakthrough started to take place. The first step began when the shock wore off and people began laughing. Jenna's revelation was so spontaneous, so delightful, and so filled with joy that every spirit present was lightened. As the laughter started, people actually started talking with each other across those invisible barriers. In fact, by the time we left that evening, we felt a real connection to everyone in that café.

The important thing to understand about this story is that living in a small town like Hamilton, we had seen every one of those people in that café before. We simply couldn't miss them in such a small town. There is only one post office, only a couple of grocery stores, and only five blocks of Main Street. But we never spoke to one of these people until that little girl created a breakthrough for all of us. Until Jenna's "heavenly burst" we would have walked by these people in our community as though they were invisible. Now when we saw these folks we'd stop, say hello, smile, and connect. It was a breakthrough of enormous proportion.

A small town is very much like the corporations and businesses in which so many of us spend so much of our time. What an exciting difference it makes to feel a sense of connection and community with the people we work with every day rather than to merely co-exist.

That day Jenna taught me that the first step in any breakthrough is vision. Breakthrough Leadership begins by focusing on solutions and possibilities instead of limits, because what you focus on is what you create.

PR—Personal Responsibility

Vision is what ignites the breakthrough process, but it's not enough. Jenna had the fresh vision that day, but it only came alive when she applied the second breakthrough leadership tool which is PR—*personal responsibility*. Personal Responsibility is the greatest birthright we've been given. We've been blessed with about nine hundred thousand hours. What we do with that gift is also called our life, also known as our personal responsibility. If Jenna hadn't taken the action to express what she saw, nothing would have changed that day.

It's the same with our lives. If we don't take the personal responsibility to stretch ourselves and take some action in the direction of our vision, then our lives will stagnate and de-energize.

The Accelerator

The last of the breakthrough tools is what I call the accelerator; it's the real fun and the real inspiration in Breakthrough Leadership. It is the power of *team.*

Yesterday I did a seminar for Lockheed Martin, one of the great companies in this country. The theme of this three-day event was "The Wizard of Oz." In preparing for this program I started thinking how I was going to tie the Oz theme into breakthrough leadership. It hit me that the most powerful message in *The Wizard of Oz* was the power of team. When you think back to Dorothy, the Scarecrow, the Tin Man, and the Cowardly Lion, the secret force that enabled them to break through all their challenges—not enough brains, not enough heart, not enough courage—was their commitment to each other. They never would have gone after the wicked witch's broomstick if they'd been alone.

That's the way it is with us. We need to have a purpose bigger than ourselves that we focus on every day. Inspired by the power of team, we're unstoppable. As an athletic coach I saw the power of that commitment to team in relay events. I saw how much better athletes did in relays than they did on their own because they were fueled by their focus on something bigger than themselves.

My breakthrough team is my family. At every one of my presentations I bring pictures of my family with me—not for everybody else to see, but to have my beloved team with me when I'm speaking. That presence gives me an inspiration that can't be matched.

So vision, personal responsibility, and the power of team are the breakthrough tools that every breakthrough requires. Building confidence, getting more done with fewer resources, bringing operations, sales, and administration into a truly cohesive, collaborative team, and igniting an unstoppable culture in your organization requires all three of those tools.

Wright

For those who are truly determined about getting things done, you propose that the power of questions is a critical ingredient. Why are questions so important to creating breakthroughs in one's life?

Biro

The term "synergy," first coined by the great thinker, Buckminster Fuller, means synthesis plus energy. When synergy is alive in your organization it means that one plus one no longer equals two. One plus one can equal fifty. Synergy is energy that comes when people work really incredibly well together.

Most of us have been raised with the belief that we go to leaders for answers. There are times when leaders need to make definitive decisions and our people depend upon our wisdom and experience. But today, real leadership—and getting more done—is much more about questions than answers. Questions create leaders, not followers. When you ask questions you put others in the position of having to think for themselves. You ignite possibility-thinking and creativity by engaging your people through the power of questions. You generate vision, personal responsibility, and the power of team by becoming what I call, a "Master-Asker"! You build an environment of mutual respect by asking for others' opinions, solutions, and strategies.

The key to becoming a Master-Asker, is that you focus on what I call, "enabling questions." There are two kinds of questions: enabling and disabling.

Examples of enabling questions are: What's the greatest team you've ever been a part of? What made it such a great team? How did you feel to be a part of that team? What did you contribute to that team? What are you truly grateful about right now? How can we accomplish this goal in record time and have fun in the process? Enabling questions enable you to focus in the direction you want to move and lead automatically to solutions that are positive, possibility-oriented, and innovative. In other words, enabling questions lead to breakthroughs!

We all ask disabling questions from time to time, especially when we get frustrated with our kids, others, or ourselves. Disabling questions lead us to focus on the obstacle or the failure. Examples of disabling questions are: Why are you so X? Why can't you ever X? Disabling questions lead to doubt, negativity, and defensiveness.

This is why it's so critical, if you want to get things done, to become a master asker of enabling questions. Enabling questions fire people's own sense of personal responsibility, they generate a higher level of team commitment and they enable people to begin to develop their vision. The secret in an organization that's getting things done is enabling everyone to know they are *all* visionaries and not to depend on only one visionary.

Wright

You often talk about living with extraordinary "E power." What is "E power" and how is that concept so important to getting things done?

Biro

I love the concept of "E power." The E stands for Energy. At the time of this interview we're having an energy crisis on our hands. I'm not just talking about the price of fossil fuels (though three dollars a gallon is pretty bad). I'm talking about the energy it takes to stay on top of everything you're asked to do professionally and then still have the energy to be fully present for your family when you come home, to take care of your health, and become engaged and involved in the things outside of work for which you have passion.

The challenge isn't that there isn't enough energy available; it's that we've been conditioned to believe that our energy is like the weather—"I hope the weather holds up for our family picnic this weekend." How often do we think the same way about our own energy? "I hope I have enough energy to get through those six meetings today and still be awake when I get home." But, the beautiful truth about the energy that unleashes your potential to get things done is that your energy is *your choice*. Energy is not like the weather—it's a matter of choice. Once you understand that you can cultivate your own energy by choice, you can elevate it to a whole new level.

I like to help people gain understanding about how they can begin to build greater energy—physically, mentally, emotionally, and spiritually. The simplest way is to gage your energy on a ten-point scale. On that ten-point scale, one is comatose, and ten is a child on Christmas morning. Using that ten-point scale, ask yourself where are you living your life? That is a magnificent enabling question.

Now, suppose you say you're living at a level seven (which would be pretty darn good compared to a lot of folks out there in the world!). How do you climb higher on that energy meter? How do you begin to cultivate the habit of greater energy?

The first key is to change the way you move. Energy is created by the way that you move. If you think of someone you know who is well into their elderly years and who seems to just keep on going like the Energizer bunny, I can guarantee you that person is one who keeps on moving. I really believe we don't get older—we just stop moving, physically, mentally, emotionally, and spiritually. When you keep moving, you keep active, you keep firing-up, and you keep getting things done at a whole different level. You stay inspired so you don't expire!

One of the best ways to move differently is to smile more. I truly believe we were meant to smile. People who get more done aren't necessarily gritting their teeth all the time. They're enjoying what they're doing. They've learned to take their job and *love* it!

The most important way to cultivate greater energy is to focus more consistently and more passionately on your *purpose*. Have you ever noticed how much energy you have when you're full of purpose? When you are fired-up by your purpose, it doesn't matter whether you've slept enough the previous week. It doesn't matter if you're not feeling 100 percent physically. When you are full of purpose, energy is no problem. But as soon as you lose sight of your purpose, it's like somebody sticks a great big pin in your energy balloon. The problem is that most people only look at their purpose on rare occasions such as New Year's Day, when they make a New Year's resolution. Looking at your purpose once a year has the same effect as going to the gym once a year. All you're going to do is get sore—it won't make a lasting difference. But if you focus on your purpose every single day by asking yourself enabling questions like, "Whom do I love and what would I change within myself to make that person's life better today?" "What's my most important next step?" and, "What am I truly grateful for right now?" you'll find yourself rising higher on your energy meter than ever before.

When you focus on your purpose consistently, you'll find that your energy becomes consistently tremendous. When you think of some of the best examples of breakthrough leaders who have truly made a difference in this world such as Jesus, Gandhi, Mother Teresa, or Martin Luther King, the amount of energy they exhibited and how much they were able to get done is astounding. As you look closely at these masters, you'll find that they had extraordinary energy because they never lost sight of their purpose—it was the key ingredient they carried with them every single day.

That kind of energy and purpose is not just available to a few special masters—it's something we all have the capacity to build within ourselves. To make your life a masterpiece, focus clearly and passionately on your purpose every single day.

Wright

You also teach that living with gratitude is vital to a winning life and getting things done. How does that affect leadership effectiveness and overall make an impact others?

Biro

When you live with an attitude of gratitude, you get a head start in the race to get things done. Instead of feeling oppressed or burdened, you look at every moment as a gift. Igniting appreciation in your spirit involves an idea that I call being a "World Class Buddy-Thanker." Again, what you focus on is what you create. Several studies of businesses have reported that we hear five to ten times more no's than yeses on a regular basis. World Class Buddy-Thankers reverse that ratio. Remember: what you focus on is what you create. It's not that World Class Buddy-Thankers are blind to reality and challenges—it's simply that they focus on what's good in people, on opportunity, and even on the seed of benefit that is planted in every adversity.

I start every single day focusing on who and what I'm truly grateful for. As soon as I ask myself what I'm grateful about in my life right now, it doesn't matter how many challenges I may be facing. By focusing on gratitude, I instantly transform my level of energy and purpose.

When you become a World Class Buddy-Thanker, and express that gratitude to others for what they bring to the table, they will run through a wall for you. They will have a much greater focus on getting things done because they feel appreciated.

Here's a fun, simple, quick way to become a World Class Buddy-Thanker—just remember ESPN:

E—Thank people with effort and energy. So often we are caught up with the rush and gush of life that we don't stop to say thank you. Stop that pattern and thank people with real sincerity and joy. We remember the moments when somebody went out of his or her way to appreciate us with effort and energy. Those moments always made us feel valued and important.

But the more surprising key to the E of ESPN is to thank people *for* their effort and energy and not just their results. We've been conditioned to only express appreciation, acknowledgement, and praise when people have achieved the goal, finished the project, or met the numbers. Though it's important to keep acknowledging people for those accomplishments, it's even more important as a breakthrough leader to thank people for their effort, their energy, and their attitude. As you thank people for their effort and energy, guess what? You will find that they will produce more results!

S—Use the power of surprise. Surprise is the least known and most magical tool to helping people get things done. For example, a hand-written card today creates surprise because we simply don't receive many hand-written cards anymore. Making that unexpected phone call to say thanks, taking an unannounced break in a regular business meeting to make an unexpected surprise acknowledgement of a teammate for some special effort or extra-mile attitude they've demonstrated inspires great loyalty and enthusiasm in others. We remember surprise. It is a very powerful, motivating, and woefully under-used form of leadership that can transform you into a World Class Buddy-Thanker.

P—Be fully Present. When you're fully present, 100 percent of your mind, body, and spirit is with the people you're with, where they are *now!* It is the secret to building trust and nothing enables others to know they are important more than when we are fully present for them. When people know they are important, they rise up to their true potential and get more things done with passion and excellence.

N—The time to become a World Class Buddy-Thanker is *now*. The time to express gratitude, acknowledgement, and praise is now, not "as soon as . . ." The road with the street sign marked "As Soon As" dead ends at the place called "Never." You may never pass this way again. When it comes to seizing the WOO, it's now, or it's gone!

Wright

What's the most important key to getting things done and becoming a break-through champion?

Biro

I think the foundational ingredient—the most important thing that you can do and focus on—is to be fully present. I just introduced the principle when we talked about ESPN. Have you ever been with someone and you know that his or her body is there, but the rest of the person is in another place? We've all experienced times when someone we truly wanted to be present was simply not there for us. And every single time we felt that lack of presence, it made us feel worthless and unimportant.

Studies have asked this important question: what do we want first and foremost from our leaders? The answer from these studies has been consistent and clear: what we want first is honesty—we want to be able to trust our leaders, to know they care and are worthy of our trust.

The way you build trust at a foundational level is by being fully present. You can't fake being present. People know instantly when your mind and your spirit is somewhere else. When you're fully present, it sends the unmistakable message to others that they matter, and that they're important. Nothing is more crucial to effective leadership than letting your people *know* that they're important.

It's just as important to take time every day to be present with *yourself* whether it's in meditation, prayer, affirmation, or some form of exercise that allows you to become quiet and free for awhile from the busy-ness that seems to constantly swallow us. It's what I call the recharge time of life. As a former swimming coach, I learned that both your on button and off button need to work efficiently for you to be really effective in getting things done.

In swimming, the underwater portion of an arm-stroke—when you're pulling the water beneath you—is called resistance. You're moving the weight of the water. I call the resistance phase of life the "doing stuff"—when we're out there making it happen. The next phase of the arm-stroke occurs once you release the water behind you and begin to lift your elbow up above the water to reach out and do the next stroke. This is called the recovery. The most important outcome of the recovery phase is to let go, relax, and refresh so you're ready for the next resistance.

The time you take to be fully present with yourself each day is the recovery phase of life where we recharge so we can get more things done.

Wright

So what are the most challenging obstacles to breaking through and getting things done?

Biro

The biggest challenge to breaking through and getting things done is that we can easily get so caught up in the rush and gush of life that we forget we have choices. We have choices about our energy, focus, and presence. When we forget that we have these choices, we begin to think we are helpless instead of empowered in our lives. But when you remember that you are a breakthrough leader, and that who you are makes a difference, you bring momentum, purpose, and value to your life.

Another big challenge to getting things done and breaking through is called blame. It's very easy to blame others or circumstances rather than to take responsibility. Responsibility is something you take. Credit is something you give. Blame is always about the past. Can you change the past? No. So as long as you stay stuck in blame, you're staying in the past. The opportunity to create a new solution is in the present that leads to a better future. It doesn't mean that people don't mess up—we all do. But a blame-buster is a person who says, "Okay, here's what happened, what are we going to do now? What are we going to learn from this? How can we improve from this? Let's get moving again instead of staying focused on the past."

Blame is probably the most insidious destroyer of teams. When you become a blame-buster and build a culture in your organization where blame has no place, you shift the focus to solutions and innovation. In such a culture people are fired-up about taking good risks. If you don't take good risks in an organization you stop moving forward. As Howard Schultz, the Chairman of Starbucks says, "Keep reinventing yourself, even when you're hitting home runs."

Wright

It's often been said that the definition of insanity is doing the same thing over and over and expecting a different result. How does that tendency keep us from getting things done and what are the keys to breaking through this challenge?

Biro

That is such an important tendency to break through. Let me ask you a question. "What color is a yield sign?" Probably 90 percent of the people reading this will think yellow. But here's the truth: yield signs have been red and white for eighteen years! We have seen thousands of yield signs and yet we haven't seen one of them for what's really there. Why? Because most of us rarely use our vision to see; instead we use our memory and our conditioning. That's why we keep doing the same thing over and over and expecting a different result. When you use your memory to see you do not see what is, you see what was.

The key to understanding how to break through the habit of doing the same thing over and over again, even though you know you have more potential, is pay attention to what you're doing, open your eyes afresh now, and if it's not working, try something different.

I sometimes have participants in my seminars do a wonderful exercise called "Bottoms Up." It's a hilarious game done with a partner. Both partners receive one simple instruction—to end up with every part of his or her body up and off the floor except hands for the count of three. As I explain the game, I demonstrate a way to do it. The demonstration I give, though, is the most difficult way to possibly do it. They see me demonstrate it with a partner once and then I say, "Play the game." Instantly everybody tries to do it exactly the way I just did it, even though it's readily apparent that it's not working. No one even thinks to try something different.

We so often do the same thing in our jobs. We keep doing things over and over again in ways that feel forced and difficult. The secret to breaking through the habit of doing the same thing over and over and expecting a different result is to ask ourselves more enabling questions like: how can we get this done in half the time, and have more fun in the process?

Wright

In your corporate career you've believed that the almost constant barrage of meetings often sapped energy and momentum from a team. To tackle that challenge you came up with something called "The Team Possibility Format." Will you tell our readers how that works and its impact on getting things done?

Biro

I'm sure that virtually every person who is in a corporate arena right now and who is reading this book knows what I'm talking about when I mention those meetings. It's obvious that we need to have meetings from time to time—they're important. But the constant barrage of meetings can become oppressive. Many meetings seem to drag on endlessly. Again it's so important to apply the principle of: if it's not working, try something different. How can we create much more momentum in meetings and get things done faster? What are the challenges with meetings?

1. They take too long.
2. Sometimes when we leave the meeting we feel that we know less than when we started because people go off on tangents.

3. Somebody dominates the meeting and we don't feel that we need to be there because we don't have any sense of ownership or participation.
4. There are too many meetings.

I came up with the Team Possibility Workshop format when I met Coach John Wooden and found out how he ran his basketball practices. He was the most successful coach in college history with ten NCAA Championships, a record that's probably never going to be broken. Yet he ran remarkably short ninety-minute practices, and his teams were better conditioned, better prepared than his competition, and seemed to peak right at the precise time of the year when the championships began. How did he pull that off? The key was the planning he put into those practices and the energy and focus that filled every one of those ninety minutes. I applied the same principles to create successful business meetings:

- Time is your friend.
- Everyone must be engaged as opposed to just one or two people.
- Everyone must know and take ownership of what they're going to do when the meeting concludes.

With these principles as a guide, the Team Possibility Meeting format was born. It consists of three simple steps:

1. Part one is brainstorming. Create your agenda in the form of a few key enabling questions. You ask those questions and set the team free to write down on flip charts or white boards all the ideas and solutions they come up with. The key to effective brainstorming is there's no assessment. You don't even praise any single idea too much because when you do that, others may be afraid their idea won't measure up and they won't speak up. You'll be amazed at how many great, powerful ideas will be brought up in ten minutes.
2. Part two is to prioritize and clarify. You spend another ten minutes where the team prioritizes the solutions that came out during the brainstorming session and makes any clarifications necessary if any of the ideas were not understood. The easiest way to prioritize is to have all the team members simply rate the ideas they consider the top five using a simple point system.

3. In the final section of the meeting the team decides who will do what by when. It's simply people taking responsibility to make those ideas happen. Volunteerism grows exponentially by this point because everyone has been engaged in the meeting process.

That simple three-part team possibility workshop format gets everyone energized and moving forward. It stimulates creative ideas, none of which are lost because all ideas are recorded. Remember that some of the ideas we initially find ridiculous and far-fetched end up creating the greatest positive change. Because you've recorded all ideas, some of those that seem "out there" become seeds that will take root at a later time. With the Team Possibility format, a meeting that normally would have taken two hours is over in thirty minutes. People are fired up, they know what to do next, and they feel like it was a good use of their time.

Wright
Today we have been talking with Brian Biro, America's Breakthrough Coach. He's one of the nation's foremost speakers and teachers of leadership, possibility-thinking, thriving on change, team-building, and getting things done. He is also author of the acclaimed bestseller, *Beyond Success.*

Brian, it's really been a pleasure for me to ask you all these questions and get all these sterling answers from you. You've helped me tremendously and I really appreciate your being with us today on *Getting Things Done.*

About the Author

BRIAN BIRO is America's Breakthrough Coach! Brian is one of the nation's foremost speakers and teachers of leadership, possibility-thinking, thriving on change, team building, and getting things done. One of his clients described Brian best when he said, "Brian Biro has the energy of a ten-year-old, the enthusiasm of a twenty-year-old, and the wisdom of a seventy-five-year old!" Brian is the author of the acclaimed bestseller, *Beyond Success,* and five other life-changing books. A former vice president of a major transportation company, Brian was rated number one from over forty speakers at four consecutive *Inc* magazine international conferences. With degrees from Stanford University and UCLA, Brian has appeared on *Good Morning America,* CNN's *Business Unusual,* and *Fox News.*

Brian Biro
1120 Burnside Dr.
Asheville, NC 28803
Phone: 828.654.8852
Fax: 828.654.8853
E-mail: bbiro@att.net
www.brianbiro.com

Chapter 11

AVA FLUTY, ND, MEd, CNHP

David Wright (Wright)

Today we're talking with Dr. Ava Fluty. Leading edge organizations are picky about the trainers they select to educate their people. They want a speaker who presents intensive, skill-packed programs with just the right amount of humor and warmth. And that's why businesses such as Gannett Newspaper, Sprint Telephone, St. John's Hospital, and Disney University, to mention a few, choose Dr. Ava Fluty to present seminars for them. Ava has the background, a master's in Administration and Supervision, a doctoral degree in Naturopathic Health, and more than twenty-five years' experience, including university levels. Ava is a developer/trainer of custom programs for private and government agencies. She has been a top ranked course leader for an international seminar company and she is one of their top ten salespeople. Dr. Ava knows how to get and keep an audience's attention and make the day a productive learning experience. She has the latest information, theories, and techniques at her fingertips. As a successful business owner of several companies, Ava understands and has firsthand experience of the necessity for your employees to be motivated, enthusiastic, and eager to lead for you. As a national/international trainer Ava has trained in Indonesia, Singapore, Hong Kong, and all over the United States on time-tested skills of leadership, communication, and service. Ava's keynotes and trainings are customized to meet your organization's specific needs. At the end of your session, you and your people will have experienced a memorable seminar that leaves you not only educated, but entertained as well.

Ava, welcome to *Getting Things Done.*

What does "getting things done" mean?

Ava Fluty (Fluty)

It means managing time and multiple priorities—having more time to do what you want to have time to do. Getting things done is how to keep all the balls in the air, all the time—easy to say but hard to do. Have you ever said, "Well, I just don't have time to do that," and turned around and made it happen? Getting things done is about choices. Time can't be managed but the choices and decisions that you make about how you use your time can. Everybody has twenty-four hours in a day, no more and no less. Everybody has 525,600 minutes a year and the only way you can gain more time is to stop doing unproductive things and put productive things in its place. That is Time Management in one sentence.

Wright

What can we do to get more done in less time?

Fluty

First, know your Prime time. Prime time is when you are potentially at your best—those times during your day when you get the most done because you have the most energy and mentally you are alert. You need to be aware of the types of activities you work on during these periods. Ask yourself, "When is my energy at its highest—morning or afternoon?" I start into my peak time around 11:00 AM, as far as thinking and processing, and I might work up to 9:00 or 10:00 PM. Most people are morning birds. These people get up, ready to think and process and they run out of steam around 4:00 PM. One is not better than the other; the important thing is to do your most important, difficult, complex, and decision-making activities during your prime time. Equally important is to know your down time—the time when your energy is "lower." Do things such as reading mail, filing, system/administrative imposed items, make phone calls, etc. If your prime time is still working mid-day, here is a tip that is worth the price of this book: go to lunch, out of the lunch cycle. Why? You will be interrupted less and getting more done because you are working while everyone is gone.

Wright

Many of us don't even consider that we have control over some of our time. Getting things done is making choices about what we do when, right?

Fluty

Yes, you have to control what you can control. Controllable time is the time left after you subtract the time spent on interruptions, unanticipated crises, and system imposed activities. Uncontrollables prevent us from working on what we planned. Controllable time is used to accomplish actions from your "to do" list. Many of us have less than 25 percent of controllable time. Scheduling too many tasks for the amount of controllable time leads to failure, frustration, stress, and guilt.

Wright

Sounds like planning would help.

Fluty

You are exactly right. If you want to manage priorities and multiple projects and get more done, you must plan. Most people are victims of momentum—the treadmill of life. Successful people plan. They are not successful by accident. To paraphrase Brian Tracy, successful people clearly know what they want and map it out; unsuccessful people never quite get it. If you want to get more done, you must plan. Planning is the thinking that precedes doing. Planning is interpreting, gathering, formulating, and examining alternatives. Planning gives leverage. A study done explained that for every one minute of planning, the time required to complete an activity is reduced by three to four minutes. Planning makes things happen. Without planning chaos reigns and events are left to chance. Effective planning ensures completion of priorities. Planning promotes job and career advancement.

Wright

Will you share with our readers some quick and easy steps to begin?

Fluty

Absolutely. Start each day and end each day with ten minutes of planning. Take a look at what needs to be accomplished, by when, who needs to be involved, and what the time line is. This will help you plan.

You need some type of system in place that you will use to keep you focused. Many people use a "tickler file" for focus and tracking. This tool is a twelve-month calendar with thirty-one days behind the month you are in. As you carry items from the in-box to your desk, one of two things should happen: either you are working on them or you are filing them. If an item does not require your immediate attention, file it in your tickler file. Here is the secret of the tickler file: you are always working one to two days ahead. Example: if this report is due January 18, I will be working on it on the 16th. That way I never miss a deadline. If this project had five people working on it, I would file it under January 13, that way, if one person has dropped the ball it gives us plenty of time to catch up.

This is also a great tracking tool. When done you insert the dated folder behind the next month. The beauty is you are always aware. If today is January 16, in my last ten minutes of planning time, I pull out the January 18 folder. I put that in the middle of my desk. Why? I have a plan for where my day will start on the 17th. That does not mean it always works; unexpected things happen, and if I have planned well, after I handle the unexpected, I do not waste time trying to figure out where to start.

Wright

Why do we put things off—procrastinate?

Fluty

William Knaus wrote that most of us learn procrastination skills in school and carry them over into the workplace. For some of us, we really do work better under pressure because it will cause us to focus and not waste time.

Most people procrastinate because they do not know where to start. Studies suggest that there are six main reasons we procrastinate: lack of clear goals, underestimating the difficulty of the task, underestimating the time required to complete the task, unclear guidelines for outcomes, feeling you have no say, and lack of planning. We've talked about that last one.

Another reason people procrastinate is because they are perfectionists. Striving for perfection can lead to major stress and set you up for failure. Learn to set realistic goals and be patient with yourself. Ask yourself the following questions: Is there an easier way to do this project? Am I spending more time than this project deserves? What are the advantages/disadvantages of doing this a more time-saving way? What have I missed due to spending too much time on this? A perfectionist can maintain high standards without it being 100 percent all the time.

Wright

Another real issue of getting things done is organization skills and prioritizing. Do you have any tools to help us with these challenges?

Fluty

The Priority Indicator or Forced Choice Tool is one of the greatest tools you'll ever learn to use, particularly if procrastination is one of your limitations. This is a great tool when *everything* is a top priority. You can't do all eight things dropped on your desk at the same time. The best tip to learn with the Priority Indicator/Forced Choice Tool is that no matter how many items are being considered, the choice is only between two at a time. Take your "to do" list and write it down the left side of the page; number each item. To the right, start at item number two. You are going to write in what appears to be fractions:

1. Monthly report – January

2. Schedule for February $\dfrac{1}{2}$

3. Call xyz client $\dfrac{1}{3}$ $\dfrac{2}{3}$

4. Check e-mail $\dfrac{1}{4}$ $\dfrac{2}{4}$ $\dfrac{3}{4}$

5. Training $\dfrac{1}{5}$ $\dfrac{2}{5}$ $\dfrac{3}{5}$ $\dfrac{4}{5}$

The idea is to compare each item on your list to each item. Don't worry about any other item except the two you are deciding between. Circle which one is most important to do first between the two. Example: Look at item number five. Compare it to item number one ($^1/_5$). Which one would be the top priority for you today, in this moment? Circle either one or five in your fraction—you have to pick one. Now compare item number two to item number five ($^2/_5$). Which one is more important to you today, in this moment? You have to pick one. Circle either number two or number five in your fraction. Do numbers three to five and numbers four to five. You do this for every item on your list. Circle the priority.

The last step is count how may times you circled each number in your fractions. The one you circled the most is your number one priority. You will rank the remaining items in order based on how many you have of each. Remember, this is only a tool to prioritize with and an especially good one for perfectionists and procrastinators.

Wright

Any tips on managing results when getting things done?

Fluty

Learn what I call the "F-A-S-T" system for priority management:

F—Focus your energies on the results you want. What is my goal? What are my roles and responsibility? Deadlines? How will I know that I have met my target? What might get worse? Resources available? Focus on finishing, not perfection.

A—Agree on priorities with boss, co-workers, etc. to clarify what these priorities are and when.

S—Schedule your day. Schedule time to plan, schedule reoccurring meeting and assignments, schedule down times, meetings, completion dates.

T—Track. Use charts, project folders, calendars, tickler files, and whatever you can to track movement to completion.

Wright

How do you determine what is greatest in importance when priorities collide?

Fluty

Let me give you some questions. Does this task require my immediate attention? How can my time be best spent in the next thirty minutes? Can this be broken down and sourced out to others? Delegation—how much time will this take? This last question is an extremely important one. Most of us underestimate time. When we estimate, we estimate what is called "pure time." That means uninterrupted time. How many of you have uninterrupted work time? Most people don't even have uninterrupted sleep time. When you estimate time, you need a new formula. If you are familiar with the task, estimate one and a half times the time, if you are unfamiliar with the task, double the time you are estimating. If it will be done during peak traffic time, double your time. Your time estimates will be closer on target.

Some other questions: Does the task contribute to my goals or the goals of the organization? Does the task hinder another goal? Who is waiting for this task? What is the deadline? What are the immediate consequences if I do not do this task now? These questions help you organize your thoughts and assess what steps need to be taken. Remember, priorities are a reflection of how you spend your time. Let me ask you a question: what activity would significantly impact your effectiveness if you did it every week for a year?

Wright

Do you have any tips for letting go of non-priority tasks?

Fluty

Start by looking at your goals. Are you doing things that support your goals? Look at your plans for the day. Do your plans support your goals? Do your plans match your goals? If not, why not? If your plans do not match your goals, adjust accordingly.

Wright

You have mentioned goals several times. How does goal-setting impact getting things done?

Fluty

Goal-setting is everything. Most people say they are goal-setters, yet when I asked some of them if they write their goals down they said, "No, I keep them in my head." Those are wishes. Goals have to be specific details of what is to be accomplished. They have to be measurable. You have to have some way of measuring success. You have to have an action plan. Goals include the realistic steps you will take. They must be doable, achievable, and timely deadlines. If you really want to get things done you need to write results-based goals: (1) What needs to be accomplished? (2) What are the anticipated results? (3) Why should it be done? (4) What steps or strategies can be used to accomplish the goal? (5) How will I keep track of what has been accomplished? Goal-setting is a must for staying on track. You have to have a clear vision of what you want to do.

Address any opposition you might have with the team, the organization, or yourself. When people become a hindrance, it is time to make them participants. What obstacles do you need to address? Be able to explain the end results of your goals, specifically, with a timeline. And the big one—put it in writing.

Wright

What other time management tools will help us get things done?

Fluty

Know and eliminate time wasters. You can't get things done if you are unaware of who and what wastes your time: telephone, people, meetings, yourself—which one is your biggest? When you are on the phone, stand. It will cut one minute off most calls. Make a list of calls, numbers, and discussion items. Group outgoing calls against automatic stop times, lunchtime, or quit time. People/visitors are a big time waster. Put your back to the traffic pattern, otherwise every time someone walks by and you look up and make eye contact, he or she will come in. Do not keep candy and other interesting things on your desk. Visit others at their desks, that way you control your time.

Another tool is called Chat and Stroll but we will save that for another book.

For meetings, have an agenda. You might think this is a commonsense item, right? Wrong! A large number of organizations, departments, and teams hold meetings out of habit. The meetings have no purpose. Meetings—another commonsense item? Not happening. Start and stop meetings on time. Assign roles of participation and tell participants what will be expected of them in the meeting.

You are a big time waster for yourself. Example: you and a coworker at break, talking about something and a name has slipped your mind. You go back to work, you are working hard and the name comes to mind. You quit doing productive things to call the coworker with an unproductive piece of information. This is called "blurting." Make a note pad for your blurts. Put all your blurts on it and make blurt calls right before the end of your work day when most people are the least productive.

I cannot quote the source but I read that this one tip will reduce self-interruptions by 90 percent, saving you three or more weeks of productive time a year. Wow, talk about getting things done! *Focus on effective actions.* Remember, I said that to get things done, stop doing unproductive things and put productive things in its place. Maximize your productive time. Know your peak time, prioritize projects, and plan. Minimize interruptions.

Wright
If I do all of this, what can I do to get commitment and cooperation from others?

Fluty
First you have to believe in the project and have enthusiasm for it. In other words, you have to sell it! To sell it you have to relate the project to the overall mission/vision of the company and tie the goals in. How you communicate this is your key to success. If you want consensus you will need to use your excellent communication skills to negotiate. Remember, people are your best asset. Keep your focus on others. A person wrapped up in himself or herself makes a pretty small package.

Wright
So what is the secret for asking for what you need?

Fluty
We are back to communication skills and knowing the personality of the people you are asking. You can not do this alone. You will have to ask for help. Be specific about what you need—don't assume others will follow a long. Draw them a picture. Be prepared—do your homework on what it will take—resources, time, money, skills. Be sure and explain how your request supports the goals of the organization. Be willing to negotiate and express appreciation for any and all cooperation.

Wright

You have given us plenty of tools to get things done. Any last thoughts?

Fluty

Getting things done is a process. It takes deliberate effort. Implement what you can *now* and plan for the future. Organization and time management takes practice and practice makes permanent!

***Content for this chapter comes from: Prioritize, Organize, The Art of Getting it Done; Peg Pickering and Organized to be your Best!; Susan Silver.

About the Author

DR. AVA FLUTY offers keynotes and training with the following advantages:

- A full range of business skills solutions
- Customized curriculum that will focus on your specific needs
- Interactive workshops and classes designed to create performance transformation
- Provide customer service that maximizes customer retention
- Create, restore, and maintain smooth communication and transfer of knowledge
- Keep teams productive and focused
- And much more!

The rules for work are changing. We are no longer judged solely by how smart we are or our level of expertise. More and more, employees need to develop a rounded set of skills to succeed in the workplace. Without the skills to perform at this new level, your staff will move at half-speed—creating bottlenecks, losing focus, causing conflict, and slowing down the entire organization.

Dr. Ava Fluty provides keynotes and trainings to address this new reality. The result is organizations that are ready for changes, that communicate effectively, that complete projects on time, that resolve conflicts, that meet and beat customer expectations, and that get out in front and stay there!

Dr. Ava Fluty, ND, MEd., CNHP
15073 Balmoral Loop
Ft. Myers, FL 33919
Office: 239.437.3672
Cell: 239.989.9535
E-mail: avafluty@aol.com
www.avafluty.com

Chapter 12

DAN MADDUX

David Wright (Wright)

Today we're talking with Dan Maddux. Dan is Executive Director of the American Payroll Association (APA), which provides education and support for more than 22,500 member professionals in the payroll industry.

Starting as its first employee in 1982, Dan has championed the Association's continuous growth and solidified its financial strength. APA trains over 18,000 professionals yearly and has 140 affiliated local chapters. He oversees APA's multiple locations, including two training and event centers in Las Vegas and San Antonio, and offices in New York City and Washington, D.C.

He created APA's National Payroll Week annual public awareness campaign and conceptualized the Knowledge Assessment Calculator, an award-winning interactive software program.

Dan, welcome to *Getting Things Done*.

Maddux

Thank you, David.

Wright

What's the difference between "childlike" and "childish" qualities and why are these concepts important to team-building and success?

Maddux

Childlike qualities are hot commodities in the workplace. People who are childlike are more likely to be resourceful and creative. Like children, they look at things with fresh eyes and are open to possibilities. They also work productively with others in all settings, whether they are leading or being led.

On the other hand, those who are childish often behave like naughty little children—they are selfish, self-centered, and upset when they don't get their way. Childish people are difficult to work with. They are roadblocks who negatively affect our overall productivity and the service we provide our customers.

We have both kinds of people in the workplace. In fact, each of us has a bit of both childlike and childish qualities within us.

As employers, we must handle instances of childish behavior quickly so they don't hinder our productivity.

Wright

Would you describe examples of how they affect your organization or projects?

Maddux

To answer your question in a broader sense, employees with childlike qualities are more successful in every task they perform. Such workers have a good attitude and are open to learning new things. They contribute to every project.

I think college degrees are overrated. Of course, people seeking to acquire specialized skills need education and everyone needs ongoing education of some type. But overall, a college degree only helps you get your foot in the door when you are pursuing an opportunity; it's not necessarily going to help you keep a job once you get it. In most cases, once you hire the right people, you can teach them what they need to know. Those childlike qualities—including resourcefulness, the ability to work well with others, and respect for their peers—are ultimately the source of success for both the employee and the employer. Higher education is important, but having practical work experiences simultaneously is a huge benefit once degree programs are completed. I think education makes more sense if applied to work experience during the same formative years.

Wright

Within your business, what is the key attribute that you look for in employees in both administration and management?

Maddux

I look for a positive attitude. I think ultimately, as long as they have a positive attitude, we can teach them. Honesty and integrity, of course, are also absolutely necessary.

We also need to realize that in business we are all selling and servicing something. So it all starts with good customer service—both internally and externally. If you don't have good customer service among the various departments within an organization, you certainly can't expect your employees to foster that with your customers.

Like customer service, diversity also starts at home. In today's economy, where we serve a diversified and often worldwide market, we need to relish diversity as part of the workplace rather than ignore it.

Wright

So why is it important to always ask, "What's in it for my customer?" How does this question help grow business?

Maddux

You can design what appears at face value as a brilliant marketing strategy, but if you haven't taken the time to ask what's in it for the customer, or economic buyer, you're really wasting your organization's time and resources. Do your homework first!

When you are creating any kind of marketing vehicle, you want to ask: "Who is the customer?" "Who is the decision-maker?" and "Who is the influencer?" And often the influencer is not necessarily the decision-maker. Or sometimes the person the product or service is intended for isn't necessarily the person who's going to receive, view, and review the ad, commercial, or brochure—someone else is making the decision. So you have to answer the question, "What's in it for the decision-makers?" If there are influencers involved as well, what is in it for them?

If you're asking a decision-maker to invest in a product or service that will ultimately benefit his or her subordinate, the decision-maker is not necessarily going to just be sold on the ROI. Ultimately, he or she is going to be looking for the ROI that more directly will affect his or her own success and position.

A mistake a lot of people make is not answering all the questions in the customer's mind. We as consumers don't give marketing and advertising much time if it doesn't quickly answer most of our basic questions and tap into some of our wants, needs, and desires.

So making sure you maximize your marketing and advertising efforts by always doing your homework first and asking: "What's in it for the customer?" "What's in it for the decision-maker?" and "What's in it for the influencer?" is extremely important.

Wright

Let's talk about architecture and design for a moment. Do you really think the space an organization inhabits has an impact on its functioning? Why is it important and how does it work?

Maddux

I believe that architectural and spatial designs are important aspects of creating positive and productive workspaces. The right space has a good floor plan and proper ergonomics, and it enhances productivity. A well thought-out space makes employees feel comfortable and helps to foster a sense of pride in where they work and who they are working for. Well-designed workspaces boost morale and create a positive work environment.

I think you want a space that disarms people and is not too rigid, but you also want an environment that creates a sense of decorum. Throughout my career I've experienced different kinds of work environments and I will tell you that one of the least productive work environments is where you have what I call the doughnut or the loop. This is where, to get from point A to point B, you have to pass nearly every open department and office. People tend to meander and they tend to stop and talk to people about things that could be better handled through e-mail and could take up a lot less time than actually making personal visits.

I like to create work environments that are departmentalized, where there is a main corridor that links all departments. This makes it very easy to identify people who waste time by wandering the corridors to visit other departments to satisfy their need for a great deal of face-to-face interaction within the workday. To battle that, create social spaces and instruct employees when socializing is acceptable. It might be first thing in the morning. Some people need that to start their day. Meal breaks, of course, would be another acceptable time.

I believe that all companies should be looking at ways to have social gatherings and celebratory activities for their employees. But those social interactions should not be happening at random times throughout the day.

Wright

So how do you approach making a major decision like buying new property?

Maddux

When buying property I think a lot of people get too involved in the aesthetics rather than the business aspect of it, while others can only look at the business aspect of it. I believe you need to gather information, do your homework, and have all the pros and cons along with the history of the property that you're looking at.

You should always have a plan. You should have a list of priorities and know why you are even considering a property purchase. Is it a long-term investment? Is it a short-term investment? Is it going to be rental property? Do you have an immediate use for it? What kind of flexibility will you need within that property? Who are your neighbors? Are they going to help or hinder your use or redevelopment of the property?

In the long run, tangible investments have always proved to be excellent investments. If you are in a property right now that you lease and that's perfect for your business, I suggest you go out and find a property that meets your investment criteria as the perfect space for your business in the future. If it already has a tenant in it, you can purchase it now and continue to lease it out. Perhaps five years from now, you might find with rent escalations that income from the rental property will have helped finance your renovations for your own purposes with the profit over expenses during the lease term. The point is, don't wait until you need to move to start looking for a new property. Plan ahead and make the acquisition with built-in income to allow time for a smooth financial transition.

Ultimately, for properties we purchase, whether it is a short-term investment or a long-term investment, I ask myself the same questions: What is our immediate purpose and long-term purpose? What is the likelihood of the neighborhood's development? Does it have built-in income? Are there any landmark or zoning issues that might restrict our flexibility in using the property? Is this a decision that is going to benefit the organization long after I'm no longer here?

Wright

It seems like you're good at seeing the potential in projects, buildings, and people. Do you think that recognizing potential is an important part of getting things done?

Maddux

Yes, recognizing potential is vital to business success. Nowhere is that skill more needed than in selecting the right job candidate.

I'm a firm believer in the interview process. I like to do interviews in the latter part of the day. We tell the candidate to come prepared not to have anywhere to go after the interview so that I have the individual's undivided attention for as long as I feel is necessary. I think that there's no way, from an initial interview, to gain enough knowledge about that individual or for him or her to gain enough knowledge about our organization. A thorough interview process takes at least two to three hours. I often often do interviews for at least two-and-a-half hours because what I'm looking for is somebody who's going to be in our employment for at least ten years.

The interview is a business transaction. I think it's the spontaneity of what happens within the second hour that truly defines the chemistry revealing whether this person is the right fit for us and vice versa.

I usually have other people within the company conduct separate interviews so I can get their feedback as well. One of the last steps we take to make sure that we're hiring the right person is to invite the individual to a social function such as a luncheon with three other people who represent a diverse cross-section of the company culture. I want to see how the candidate interacts with others.

I take a lot of pride in the fact that we have great diversity within our company, which has only ninety employees. As I mentioned earlier, since we work in a global economy, being comfortable with all aspects of diversity is essential, both internally and externally.

Wright

You have been described as having the ability to find the win-win in every circumstance—someone who values people, treats them with dignity, and sees the talent in each of them. Is that positive attitude you've been speaking about an important part of getting things done?

The question would be, don't you have to be critical to get things done?

Maddux

You do have to have good critical judgment to get things done, but that doesn't necessarily mean your critical judgment should sponsor or encourage negativity. It is useful to look at things from a broader perspective—the bird's eye view. I think that one of the most important things to do as a leader is to leave your ego at the door.

If a supervisor or CEO is too excitable or too quick to get upset in certain situations, it truly rattles the cages of employees and wastes a huge amount of time in lost productivity because everyone is waiting to see how the boss reacts. By being more even-tempered and by being a pleasant, supportive person, you set the proper tone, the proper decorum.

Often people who experience bad boss behaviors or have had bad bosses in their careers feel overwhelmed by it, and too often they never take the time to dissect the experience. It's a valuable lesson waiting to be learned. Ask yourself if you were ever in that same situation, what decision would you make, and what would you do differently?

Analyzing others' mistakes is one of the best ways you can learn on your road to earning management responsibilities.

As a leader, what I've tried to do is to guide people. I don't want them to be part of the problem; I want them to be part of the solution. It's all about building a solid team and treating your employees with dignity and respect. Dignity and respect should be prevalent at all employee levels. That attitude builds trust and elevates morale throughout the organization. And that is a win-win situation for everyone.

Wright

What have you learned from observing the best types of managers or bosses? What characteristics do you admire and would strive to emulate?

Maddux

I think one of the most important things I've learned is whether you travel one hour or twenty hours to participate in a meeting, whether in front of two or two hundred people, whether you are going to be there for two hours or two days, if the people you are going to see don't feel like you are completely engaged and that this is the most important thing to you at this point in time, it leaves everybody with a feeling that something is missing. You were there but you really weren't present.

I keep a very busy schedule. I travel among multiple locations. We have 140 APA local chapters across the United States. We have affiliations with organizations around the world, and I have a lot of other involvements in my business and personal life. Whether it is a social occasion like spending time with a friend I haven't seen in awhile or a meeting in front of a group, for that moment, however short or long it may be, I owe it to myself and I owe it to them to give my complete attention and be engaged in the moment.

The same thing goes for managing people. If you set up a two-hour or a two-minute meeting, you owe those attending that meeting your undivided attention. In this way, you can guide them not only to handle the task at hand but hopefully to grow professionally and learn from your behavior.

The point is, even amid our busy, hectic lives, we need to slow down and be completely engaged in the present. Know when it's inappropriate to check your BlackBerry! The best leaders have this ability and I strive to practice it in my personal and professional life.

Wright

What do you think are the three most important things leaders must do to be successful?

Maddux

I think there are many things that leaders need to do to be successful, but to focus internally, success depends heavily on the quality of your employee team.

First, the leader must select the right people for the team. As mentioned earlier, ideal employees are honest, flexible, accountable, quick learners, and team players.

Second, leaders must be able to determine their employees' strengths and give them duties and responsibilities that are right for them. Even when they don't know where their greatest talents lie, it's up to the employer to seek and discover those talents. You want to position your employees to succeed so they can contribute to your organization's success. External roadblocks will always exist; employers need to get rid of the internal roadblocks to be successful.

Third, leaders should stretch their employees. This involves training them, providing new challenges, and adding greater responsibilities so they can develop their careers. This in turn fosters a sense of accomplishment, which contributes to high morale.

Wright

What are the key factors in creating positive and productive employees and teams?

Maddux

To have productive employees, I think companies need to provide some structure. This comes from having an organization chart as well as an employee manual specifying company policies that are fairly implemented. With these items in place, employees' roles will be clearly defined. And it will help eliminate those childish behaviors we spoke about earlier.

We need to create an environment of honest communication and mutual respect among employees at all levels.

Training is also necessary to enhance the employees' ability to perform professionally. And I believe that employee education should include financial training—and more than just promoting awareness of all the benefit programs available to employees. For younger employees, the training should include the importance of budgeting, saving money, and concepts such as compounded interest. For more senior employees, financial training should include retirement planning and meeting health and long-term care expenses.

I believe doing these things will create a more engaged and more productive worker.

Wright

The APA is now twenty-five years old. Where do you see it twenty-five years from today?

Maddux

Well, I certainly see APA having many more members and services than we offer today! One thing that makes us different from many non-profit organizations is that membership fees account for only about 18 percent of our annual revenue. The majority of our revenue is derived from our education programs and publications. This has been a good business model that we will continue to develop in the years ahead. We continue to explore new avenues for delivery of services, information, and education.

Beyond taking education, publications, and services for the payroll industry to a higher level, we will continue to make investments in products and services that benefit the payroll industry and that we can also resell to other industries. A great example is our two multimedia and event centers in San Antonio and Las Vegas. While we use our state-of-the-art centers for our own training and events, we also rent them to other organizations that require similar environments to train and entertain their employees and customers. In 2007, we will open a new, state-of-the-art venue in Las Vegas called MEET. While MEET serves our purposes, it will also be another great revenue opportunity outside of our core products and services aimed at the payroll industry.

We work in a global economy so of course we want to maintain productive relationships with our global partners, including other associations of payroll and related industry professionals and government and regulatory agencies around the world. We will also want to scan the globe to identify corporations and individuals who will benefit from our services. Some of these opportunities might require delivery through more than one language. We are always looking for new ways to expand our business by traditional and nontraditional methods. It all comes back to building up and out, but on a foundation that was created to handle and facilitate growth opportunities and new revenue streams.

To grow in the future, you have to do more than think outside the box—you have to get rid of the box.

Wright

Today we've been talking to Dan Maddux. He is the Executive Director of the American Payroll Association, which provides education and support for more than 22,500 member professionals in the payroll industry. As we have found here today, he has championed the Association's continuous growth and solidified its financial strength. The APA trains over 18,000 professionals each year and has 140 affiliated chapters nationwide.

Dan, thank you so much for taking this time with me to answer all these questions; it has certainly been enlightening for me and I am sure it will be for our readers. Thank you.

Maddux
Thank you, David.

About the Author

DAN MADDUX is Executive Director of the American Payroll Association (APA), an organization that services and represents more than 22,500 payroll industry professionals through education and training, print and electronic publications, certification programs, and advocacy before government agencies. Dan is the visionary and driving force behind the success and continuous growth of the APA, with multimedia training and event centers in San Antonio and Las Vegas, including operations in New York City and Washington, D.C. Among his key accomplishments, he created National Payroll Week (NPW), a public awareness campaign to recognize the contribution of taxpayers who support our nation's economy and payroll professionals who make the payments on their behalf. Looking toward its twelfth year, NPW has been endorsed by U.S. Presidents, Congress, and government agencies and is heavily covered in the media. Dan also conceptualized the Knowledge Assessment Calculator, an award-winning interactive software program that tests the knowledge base of an organization's employees, customers, or members. Dan has hosted a syndicated radio show on employment issues that reached three million listeners, and he is frequently quoted in the radio, television, and print media. While maintaining residences in New York City, San Antonio, and Las Vegas, Dan travels extensively worldwide speaking on behalf of the APA as well as other professional groups.

Dan Maddux
American Payroll Association
660 N. Main Ave., Suite 100
San Antonio, TX 78205
Phone: 210.226.4600 ext. 2304
Fax: 210.886.9185
E-mail: danmaddux@msn.com
www.danmaddux.com
www.americanpayroll.org